Crafting Change

CRAFTING CHANGE

HANDMADE ACTIVISM, PAST AND PRESENT

Jessica Vitkus

Farrar Straus Giroux
New York

Farrar Straus Giroux Books for Young Readers
An imprint of Macmillan Publishing Group, LLC
120 Broadway, New York, NY 10271 • fiercereads.com

Our books may be purchased in bulk for promotional, educational, or
business use. Please contact your local bookseller or the Macmillan Corporate
and Premium Sales Department at (800) 221-7945 ext. 5442 or by email at
MacmillanSpecialMarkets@macmillan.com.

Library of Congress Cataloging-in-Publication Data is available.

First edition, 2022

Book design by Trisha Previte
Printed in China

ISBN 978–0–37431–332–6 (paperback)

1 3 5 7 9 10 8 6 4 2

To my daughters, Sadie Robin and Matilda Wren,
so you might share my love of art and love of country.

Table of Contents

Beyond Basic Crafts

Project How-Tos

Crafting Change from Here On: Now What? 189

Acknowledgments 192
Image Credits 193
About the Author 194

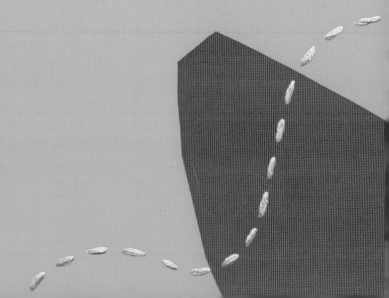

WHY THIS BOOK?

Maybe it's time to speak your truth and get your hands dirty. I don't just mean that metaphorically. Maybe you want to become politically active and need a place to start. Maybe you want to do more than click "like" on social media. The good news? You don't have to be voting age, you don't have to stand up in front of a big crowd and give a speech. Honestly, you don't even need to leave your house. You can make a difference by crafting things with your hands. This book is about people who do just that. I find them inspiring, and I hope you do, too.

MY CRAFTING BACKSTORY

I'm a longtime crafter. My grandmother taught me how to knit and crochet when I was maybe seven years old. Whenever my grandma sat on the couch, she'd pick up her project—an afghan, a sweater vest, a crochet purse I'd asked for—and start stitching. Barely looking at her hands. This, to her, was resting. I have squirrelly hands, too. My grandmother died a few years ago, at age ninety-eight. The scarves and potholders she made me are still in heavy rotation in my household. My grandma expressed love through crafting. And I still feel her love even though she is gone. There is nothing more old-school, traditional craft-y than wrapping myself in a grandma-made blanket or shawl. It's like a hug.

A shawl my grandma crocheted for me. I wear it with summer dresses.

While my grandma taught me the yarn arts, I taught myself embroidery, quilting, and hand sewing. This was pre-internet, so I learned from books and experiments—and failures. When I was about ten, I wanted to make my own Halloween costume. I thought I could be a cool octopus if I sewed extra arms onto my black turtleneck. So I stuffed a bunch of black knee socks to form tubes and stitched four of these sock-arms across my back. I put two more sock-arms front and center on my chest, which looked like a pair of long, dangly boobs. The teenage trick-or-treaters (Why were they trick-or-treating at that age?) got a biiiiiig laugh out of my costume. But, hey, I still got candy. After that, I spent more time thinking through my designs, often drawing them first. I learned to work a sewing machine in my eighth-grade home economics class. In my suburban public school, home ec (cooking and sewing) and shop class (woodworking and tool use) were electives. But almost all the girls took home ec, while the boys took shop. I didn't question the sexism back then. But years later, I did learn to operate a band saw. So . . . ha! Take that, patriarchy!

These days, I'm into hand stitching of all kinds. I sew during car rides with my family, or while watching TV. I find the repetition of stitches soothing, like touching prayer beads. I love the sound and feel of thread pulling through fabric. I always have about three needlework projects piled up next to my couch (like my grandmother did). Mending, embroidery, quilting, maybe even a little knitting. My seven-year-old daughter asked me to knit a blanket for her stuffed mouse. I'm not great at playing pretend with my kids, but I can knit a mouse blanket. So I guess crafting is my love language, too. Just like it was for my grandma. Notice how none of this is political? I'm getting there.

A CRAFTIVIST (ME) IS BORN

By day, I'm a journalist and TV producer. I direct comedy sketches and mini-documentary bits for a late-night talk show. I like to think that I help people process the day's stories, what's going on in politics and culture. I've been working in TV news and comedy for more than twenty years. To me, it's a form of activism to make fun of people in power who deserve it, to point out the ridiculous, to praise unlikely heroes. I love my country, so this is kind of a love language, too.

Years ago, when George W. Bush was president, I had an idea that made me laugh. A visual joke I wanted to sew: the Department of Homeland Security Blanket (it will not protect you in an emergency). I made a quilt with the colors and text from the actual threat level chart put out by our government's Homeland Security Advisory System. It was the first time I combined handicrafts and political humor. Two different parts of my brain working together. It was *so much fun* to make. Extremely satisfying.

Quilts are normally cozy and comforting, like my grandma's blankets, right? But not this one. The sweetness of a quilt bumping up against the scariness of a military warning creates tension. I love that tension. It's energizing. My craft-y take on a "security blanket" appeared in a political magazine in 2007 and—ta-da—I officially became a craftivist. Hopefully, my Department of Homeland Security Blanket prompted some questions like, "Hey, is this whole rainbow-striped chart a real thing in our government? If so, who decides the threat level? And how is that helpful?" In 2011, the US government got rid of the color-coded Homeland Security Advisory System. Coincidence? Probably. But I did use art to shine a light on something that wasn't working.

Department of Homeland Security Blanket: It will not protect you in an emergency.

WHAT IS CRAFTIVISM?

In 2003, maker and writer Betsy Greer put the term "craftivism" ("craft" + "activism") on the map with her craftivism.com website, and later with her inspiring book *Craftivism*. I love the term "craftivism" for its accessible grassroots feel. But even before "craftivism" was a word, regular people have been making stuff for a cause.

Embroidered graffiti with a message, spotted in Emeryville, CA

There's the AIDS Memorial Quilt, which started in the 1980s and is still growing. There were citizens (mostly women) who knit socks and bandages for soldiers in WWI and WWII. (Actually you can still knit for soldiers.) People have silkscreened T-shirts, photocopied zines, made nature sculptures, slapped posters onto walls, and recycled garbage into art. That's all craftivism, of a kind.

HELLO, LET ME BE YOUR GUIDE

For years, I've been on the lookout for other activists getting their craft on. I've been scrolling and scanning and getting inspired every day. Sometimes I see craftivism while just walking around, like a handmade statement on the back of a jean jacket. Or the graffiti of artist SacSix on the walls and lampposts of my East Village NYC neighborhood. Now he's profiled in this book.

Somebody posted their embroidered statement onto a telephone pole in Emeryville, California. Once you start noticing, you can't stop noticing.

I want to share that feeling of noticing and discovery with you. I want to be your guide, your on-ramp, your introduction to craftivism. When I was in college, I made mixtapes of my favorite songs for friends. This book is my mixtape for you. A sampler I want to share. I've selected some of the greatest hits and some deeper cuts. All gorgeous examples of political crafting in America, past and present. The list is not complete. My choices are subjective. But this is a good place to start if you are interested in art, crafts, politics, and the people who weave them together. I interviewed over a dozen makers and scholars. I found out how they got started. How they came to connect art and American politics. What do they want to change? How can crafts make a difference? How can others—whose hands and hearts are ready—pitch in?

HOW TO USE THIS BOOK

This book is a craftivism starter kit. Hop around the different chapters and read what's interesting to you. Treat it more like a cookbook or a travel guide than a history book—though there are bits of history here, too. You can focus on the issues that move you most, or get to know the different art-activists. See how they think and operate. Cara Levine hosts workshops where people sculpt clay iPhones, hairbrushes, wrenches, and other objects that have been mistaken for guns. Michael Reynolds fights climate change by building zero-waste homes that look like spaceships. Shannon Downey hosts stitch-alongs where she embroiders political messages that are as sharp as her needles. Guillermo Galindo collects objects migrants have abandoned along the US-Mexico border and turns them into sonic devices that make heart-breaking music. Politics can connect to handicraft in ways that use more of your senses—sight, sound, touch. Ways that go deeper than reading a newspaper.

If you are interested in getting involved as a craftivist (and I hope you are), then read about projects you can join in and try. You can still knit a Pussyhat. Pussyhat Project co-creator Jayna Zweiman explains what the pink hats mean to her. If you are a quilter, read about Sara Trail of the Social Justice Sewing Academy, who helps people express themselves through fabric. She has a call out for volunteers to quilt memorial panels from home.

Becca Rea-Holloway, aka The Sweet Feminist, gets debates going by posting pictures of her cakes frosted with messages unlike anything you've seen on a cake before. What if you tried that at your next school bake sale?

So, meet these art-activists I've custom picked. You don't need to agree with everyone's politics, but I hope you'll admire their work, their passion, their innovation. Follow them on their journeys. Maybe start one of your own.

DO YOU WANT TO CRAFT CHANGE?

Our nation needs help. Our environment is in crisis. Racism here is deep, systemic, and dangerous. Red states and blue states cannot work together. School shootings are still so common that even little kids have lockdown drills. Families go bankrupt without medical insurance to pay their bills. I know so many young people who feel frustrated about all this, don't feel heard, don't know what to do. This book began as an answer to the question, "How can you bring about change or have a voice when you are too young to vote?"

The craftivists in this book have all taken action in different ways. They raise awareness. They raise money. They help unite groups. Sometimes their handiwork is just a simple practical solution—like knitting socks for soldiers or building houses that don't require fuel. But all these makers have advice on how to get started, tips for beginners who are ready to stitch or sculpt or bake for a cause. Neatness does not count. Craftivism is fun, satisfying, and it serves a larger purpose. So why not give it a try?

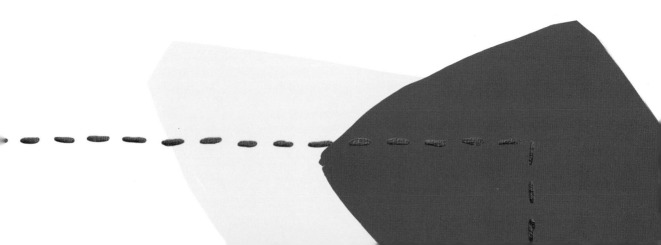

Embroidery

Embroidery

Embroidery—the art of stitching onto fabric with needle and thread—is traditionally just pure ornamentation. If someone says you are "embroidering a story," it means you are adding extra details to make it more interesting. Exactly. Embroidery has been around almost as long as fabric. Ancient Egyptian tomb paintings show embroidered clothes. In the Middle Ages, Byzantine artisans embroidered with gold. China, India, and African countries all have rich traditions of embroidery that go back centuries. In Northern Europe, up until the Renaissance, embroidery was mainly used to make fancy church garments even fancier. That upscale tradition is one of the reasons I love using embroidery to support social justice and to express very down-to-earth ideas.

In these next chapters, you'll meet two craftivists who use embroidery to bring people together in sewing circles. Irreverent and funny, they both have fine motor skills to die for. Melissa Blount embroiders to amplify messages about social injustice, and to shine a light on women that we dare not forget. Shannon Downey of Badass Cross Stitch, with her background in marketing and ready wit, has a knack for stitching her truth, and provoking thought in the very best way.

Some say the pen is mightier than the sword. I say the needle is sharper than the pen.

Chapter One
Being Blount
(2017–present)

Clinical psychologist by day, Dr. Melissa Blount expresses her own anger and feelings through stitching. Then she lets her beautiful embroidery work for justice.

Melissa Blount, art-activist who embroiders names and faces so we remember them

BLACK GIRL MAGIC PORTRAITS

I first fell in love with Melissa's work through her Black Girl Magic portraits—a series of embroidered pictures of accomplished Black women, one for each letter of the alphabet. (This structure is called an "abecedarium," or alphabet primer, with an image for each letter.) I love Melissa's clear, strong lines and sure hand—as strong as the women she's stitching. Look at Josephine St. Pierre Ruffin (1842–1924), who worked for women's rights, fought against slavery, and, as Melissa says in her Instagram post, "created the first national newspaper dedicated to the civil and cultural development of Black women." Based in Boston, Josephine was upset about the network of all-white national women's clubs, so she started a network of clubs for Black women. She accomplished all of that while raising four kids.

Since there are twenty-six letters in the alphabet, Melissa made twenty-five more portraits of notable Black women. She embroidered them on inexpensive dish towels, a deliberate choice. Melissa explains, "The dish towels are a juxtaposition to how racism has relegated Black women to the idea of servitude, domestic. Always the mammy or sassy sapphire. The women I've highlighted are no one's maid or servant." The portraits are an attempt to right a wrong, one embroidery at a time. "It's just blowing my mind. Why don't I know about these women? Why is this not in the broader culture? I've been so enlightened and inspired by their stories. But at the same time, I'm incredibly disheartened by the way Black women's humanity has been shrinking and ignored or erased." Reading about the women in Melissa's series, I think about how so many white women from history are portrayed in books and film again and again while so many Black women are overlooked. Honestly, I do not need to see another kids' book about Amelia Earhart (though she's cool).

Melissa's portrait of Josephine St. Pierre Ruffin (1842–1924), a pioneer in publishing

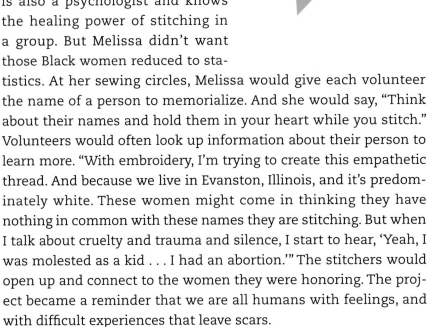

FROM DARKNESS TO LIGHT

Melissa started her joyful, celebratory alphabet series because her spirit needed it. "The women were born out of my first textile piece, which was the Black Lives Matter Witness Quilt." For that project, Melissa organized community sewing circles, where people came together to embroider the names of Black women and girls killed from January 2016 to May 2017 in Chicago. "Fifty to sixty percent of women on that quilt were killed by their intimate partners," says Melissa, who is also a psychologist and knows the healing power of stitching in a group. But Melissa didn't want those Black women reduced to statistics. At her sewing circles, Melissa would give each volunteer the name of a person to memorialize. And she would say, "Think about their names and hold them in your heart while you stitch." Volunteers would often look up information about their person to learn more. "With embroidery, I'm trying to create this empathetic thread. And because we live in Evanston, Illinois, and it's predominately white. These women might come in thinking they have nothing in common with these names they are stitching. But when I talk about cruelty and trauma and silence, I start to hear, 'Yeah, I was molested as a kid . . . I had an abortion.'" The stitchers would open up and connect to the women they were honoring. The project became a reminder that we are all humans with feelings, and with difficult experiences that leave scars.

The finished Black Lives Matter Witness Quilt was a triumph. "But I was literally physically exhausted by that project. So I asked myself, what was the flip side?" Melissa was looking for a way to celebrate Black women's lives, maybe think a little less about death. Around that time, Melissa's graphic designer husband was working on a piece about Zora Neale Hurston's poetry. Melissa wanted to embroider Zora's portrait, and the Z of Zora's beautiful name was a perfect letter for an alphabet series. The end of the alphabet was the beginning of a whole new project.

HOW MELISSA GOT INTO NEEDLEWORK

Melissa became an embroiderer as an adult, proof that you're never too old to learn new art forms. You can start whenever. "My mom laughs because she's been cross-stitching and crafting all my life. And I shunned anything craft oriented."

Melissa actually came to embroidery by way of knitting. After earning her PhD in clinical psychology at Western Michigan University in 2001, Melissa got a job at Chicago State University. She remembers, "I hated meetings. In those committee meetings I'd get so enraged, thinking, 'If I don't learn how to do something, I'm gonna kill somebody.' So I learned to knit." Not only did she learn to knit but, "I started researching the impact any handwork activity had on the body." As a therapist, she noticed and then studied the therapeutic value of needlework and crafting.

A few years later, Melissa worked at an elementary school on Chicago's South Side. "And I started a knitting class with girls and boys. The boys were like, 'That's girls' work,' and I told them, 'No, it's not. Men make clothes.' They reluctantly did it. They paid attention and they loved it, and unprompted, told me how it helped control their anger."

FIRST EMBROIDERED PORTRAIT

After a few years, Melissa fell out of her knitting habit. Mostly. ("I occasionally dipped in and out of craft stores.") But around 2009, she took an embroidery class, learning from her friend who owned a craft shop. "Then I did a piece for [my husband,] Ben. I made a portrait for Father's Day of him and our daughter." Melissa was hooked. Clearly a talented artist, she found a new medium for self-expression. "I just do one stitch, and I just try to figure out the look that I want. I do a backstitch and maybe a split stitch." But hey, you only need one pen to draw, and you only need one stitch to embroider.

FROM CRAFT TO CRAFTIVISM

I ask Melissa how her stitching turned into a form of protest. When did her craft become craftivism? "It was gradual," Melissa explains. "I always thought of Ben as the artist. But around 2014, when Michael Brown [an unarmed Black man shot by police in Ferguson, Missouri,] or Tamir Rice [a twelve-year-old Black boy shot by police at a playground in Cleveland, Ohio,] was killed—I can't even keep up with the names—Ben and I were trying to figure what we could do. We were trying to distribute these Black Lives Matter signs. People were getting into arguments about it, saying the sign was a lazy way to get involved in the BLM movement. But I thought, 'We are doing a human rights marketing campaign visually saying BLM is incredibly important.' So we started layering the city with signs."

That got Melissa thinking about "the power of words and imagery." She tells me, "If these words have such impact, putting words on textile pieces has a huge impact." So she started to think of herself as an art-activist. "It was a combination of all these things. Where my talents lie and what I am willing to do."

Health is another factor in Melissa's craftivism. "When I was forty-one, I was diagnosed with heart disease, so I can't go to the protests. It's too risky. This is the way I can protest. I can take some words and embroider them."

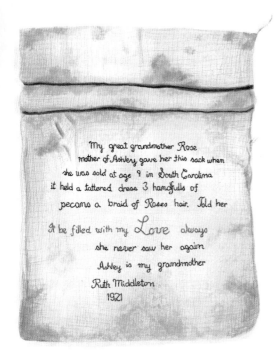

My great grandmother Rose
mother of Ashley gave her this sack when
she was sold at age 9 in South Carolina
it held a tattered dress 3 handfulls of
pecans a braid of Roses hair. Told her
It be filled with my Love always
she never saw her again
Ashley is my grandmother
Ruth Middleton
1921

Ashley's Sack is an important antique textile that tells the story of an enslaved mother separated from her daughter.

ASHLEY'S SACK

"There's an embroidered piece that a mother gave to her daughter, that had a huge impact on me," says Melissa. "It's called Ashley's Sack." In the mid-1800s, an enslaved mother, Rose, gave her nine-year-old daughter, Ashley, a sack of things to remember her by. Ashley was sold away and never saw her mother again. Ashley's granddaughter embroidered the simple cotton sack, telling this story. It illustrates the power of the embroidered word. The piece sparked an idea for Melissa, a craftivism project for the future: "I'm going to have mothers who are incarcerated embroider their letters onto feed sacks. Since mass incarceration is just the evolution of slavery."

HATERS WILL HATE

"All you are doing is embroidering, what difference does that make?" is something Melissa has heard over the years. But when the Cardi B song "WAP" came out in the summer of 2020, Melissa got stitching. "I did a piece on that. Except mine said, 'What About Prosecuting the COPS that killed Breonna Taylor?'" Melissa put it up on social media, "and people lost their minds. It is the most provocative piece I have done." Reactions ranged from, "Why would you want to link yourself with them?" to "This is so fantastic! I'm so glad you're using the hype to bring attention to Breonna Taylor." Melissa was surprised but also happy. The piece was meant to spark discussion and get attention. "So anyone who thinks this is just putting floss on a textile piece is sadly mistaken. It's amazing to me."

BREONNA TAYLOR

Breonna Taylor, a twenty-six-year-old Black woman, was the first person in her family to graduate from high school. She was interested in medicine and health care, so she became a full-time emergency medical technician in Louisville, Kentucky. But on March 13, 2020, the police acted on a tip related to a drug case involving Breonna's ex-boyfriend. He lived in another house, miles away. Three white officers raided Breonna's home, using a battering ram to break down her door. Whether or not they

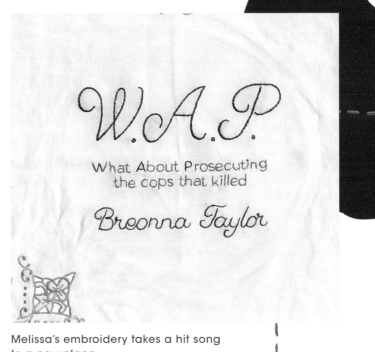

Melissa's embroidery takes a hit song to a new place.

announced themselves as police is in dispute. Breonna's boyfriend, Kenneth Walker, who was there that night, thought an intruder was attacking, so he got his registered gun and shot an officer in the leg. The police then fired at least ten rounds blindly into the apartment. Breonna was shot five times and died at the scene. There were no drugs in the apartment.

That night seemed to illustrate the racism and police violence that would become even clearer with the killing of George Floyd later that spring. There were protests in Louisville for months, and protests in several cities on the anniversary of Breonna's death. One officer was fired and charged with wanton endangerment for shooting blindly and putting the neighbors at risk. Louisville banned "no-knock" warrants. But protestors, athletes, and celebrities of all kinds (including Oprah, who put Breonna on the cover of O magazine) are still calling for justice in the form of greater consequences.

About six months after Breonna's killing, her family settled a wrongful-death lawsuit with the city of Louisville, Kentucky. Officials agreed to award Breonna's family $12 million, plus a promise that police procedures would change to help prevent tragedies like this in the future. The changes? Stricter requirements and reviews before a search warrant is approved, a better system to flag officers who use excessive force, and an ambulance nearby when conducting a raid. These seem like common sense changes, but there are still no criminal charges of murder, or even manslaughter, against any of the three white officers who conducted the botched raid. That's in the hands of the Kentucky attorney general, Daniel Cameron.

First Breonna postcard I stitched,
but not the last

THE BREONNA POSTCARD PROJECT

"I'd been thinking about it for a long time. I thought about doing birthday cards for Breonna," which is what got Melissa thinking about embroidering on paper. "Then I thought, okay, it's been six months and this fucker has not charged them yet. This guy spoke at the RNC." That fucker is Attorney General Daniel Cameron, who also spoke at the Republican National Convention in the summer of 2020. Melissa called for craftivists to embroider Breonna's name onto a postcard and send it to Cameron. Many answered the call, including me.

Not only does this project send a message to the Kentucky attorney general, but Melissa points out, "Think of the many hands the postcards pass through. Think of all the people who will see Breonna's name."

Melissa also called on people to send Breonna postcards to the mayor of Louisville or to Kentucky senator Mitch McConnell. "My goal is to shame them into good behavior. I'm a therapist and you're never supposed to shame people. Humiliation should never be part of the process. But these people don't seem to be prompted until put on blast. So that's what I'm trying to do." Sometimes you just get angry enough to break your own rules. "Often my work is fueled by rage," says Melissa. "It makes me feel better and it makes me feel empowered, and I love the immediacy of it. I can come up with a project and I can just go for it."

Melissa hosted a socially distanced (during the COVID-19 pandemic) postcard sewing event on September 13, 2020. Other craftivists hosted simultaneous online stitch-ins. At least 100 postcards were made that day. Thanks to social media, the call for Breonna postcards kept going throughout 2020, into 2021 and beyond. There's no way to

Melissa says, "Think of the many hands postcards pass through. Think of all the people who will see Breonna's name."

know how many cards were sent to the Kentucky AG's home, but he probably noticed.

Melissa says, "Out of the Breonna Project, I've started hosting a John Lewis Good Trouble Sewing Circle." John Lewis was a long-time civil rights activist and Democratic representative for Georgia until his death in 2020. He called his political activism "good trouble." Melissa continues, "A few of the women from the sewing circle helped me organize the Breonna Taylor Jump Off." Breonna Taylor liked to jump rope, double-Dutch style. So Melissa and her stitching crew organized a day of double-Dutch jumping. Another way to celebrate Breonna's life joyfully while fighting the injustice of her death.

THE POWER OF ONE

I ask Melissa what I ask myself all the time: How can one person change things? She says, "Look at the difference that George Floyd has made in death. His little girl said, 'Daddy changed the world.'" But as an artist, you have a different kind of power. "Eighty-nine cents is what a skein of floss costs. A set of napkins is three dollars, maybe five dollars for antiques, and I have the capacity to make someone who has never met me so mad because I'm telling the truth."

Chapter Two

Badass Cross Stitch

(2013–present)

Shannon Downey and her Badass Cross Stitch projects raise consciousness, provoke thought, and bring people together in a new kind of sewing circle.

2017 Women's March sign speaks for itself.

BADASSERY GONE VIRAL

Artist-activist Shannon Downey has a way of boiling down a political moment to its essence with beauty and humor. She embroidered a sign—actually a giant embroidery hoop—for the January 2017 Women's March. And it went viral for its awesomeness. It was not the only time Shannon's art burned up the internet.

In 2016, the 2005 *Access Hollywood* audiotape surfaced, catching Donald Trump saying into a hot mic that he liked to "grab 'em by the pussy." Shannon

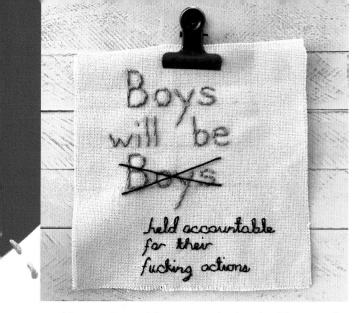

Shannon's most famous work of embroidery—so far

responded by making her "Boys Will Be Boys" piece. Then in the fall of 2017, sexual assault accusations against movie producer Harvey Weinstein became news and the #MeToo movement caught fire. Women used that hashtag in huge numbers to post about their own sexual harassment and assault. Shannon's "Boys Will Be Boys" embroidery went viral, too. Celebrities reposted it. Shannon's handmade art captured a mood. Perfectly. Shannon posted it again on February 24, 2020—the day Harvey Weinstein was found guilty.

In 2019, Shannon gave a great TED talk about white women and privilege and activism that helped open my eyes to my own behavior. (Find it on YouTube.) I've been a Badass Cross Stitch fangirl for years, so I was happy to actually talk to Shannon about her work.

ARTIST PROVOCATEUR

I start by asking Shannon an important question: What is Badass Cross Stitch? Like, is it her superhero name? Is it her brand? "That's just my art name," she explains. "I'm not a business. Not commodifying it. It's my name digitally. A fusion of activism and my art and my writing. I'm inspiring others to take action, and also driving that action. Everything I do is about pushing people, challenging, agitating. Trying to figure out what motivates people and what will engage them. As opposed to armchair activism. Like signing a meaningless online petition."

Yes, sometimes social media activism feels like a whole lot of preaching to the converted. An echo chamber. But Shannon has somehow figured out how to be an effective activist both online and in the real world.

DIGITAL/ANALOG BALANCE

Speaking of screen time, I first learned the term "digital/analog balance" from Shannon's Badass Cross Stitch site. Now I think about it every single day. I ask Shannon to help explain what it means. "In school, I got a master's in Leisure Studies (yes, that's a real thing). I studied cultural patterns and how people use their time and what motivates them. People talk about 'work/life balance' but that feels like an antiquated idea because of technology. I was running a digital marketing company and was burnt out because I was connected to a screen 24/7. That's how I got into stitching. It really transformed how I was feeling about everything. You use a different part of your brain and your body. 'Digital/analog' is the balance we need to talk about. That's a more productive conversation. I mean, tech is not going away. And I love my tech. But it's impacting young people."

BREAKING PHONE ADDICTION

"Our phone has become an additional appendage, and we feel anxious when we are not holding it or don't have it in sight." Shannon tells me how she recently tried to teach her students to meditate. (She teaches marketing and entrepreneurship at a college.) Shannon asked her students to leave their phones in the corner while she led a guided meditation. "And they were the most anxious I've ever seen. So, the next time I brought embroidery supplies and let them embroider. I had them pick a word—like 'breathe' or 'relax'— to stitch." At the end of the class, Shannon's students said they felt calm, centered. "And I told them, 'Yes, I gave you an activity to focus on. It freed you from being anxious about your phone, because your hands have a thing to do. Anybody who wants to stitch through my class, you are totally welcome to.'"

HOW HER CRAFTIVISM BEGAN

Shannon Downey, embroidery activist and provocateur

Shannon learned to embroider in fifth grade, when assigned to make a pink bunny. She was NOT into it. "To this day," says Shannon, "I don't tell people what to stitch. I don't let the content ruin the medium." Then in 2013, Shannon rediscovered stitching as an antidote to screens. "The first thing I stitched was Captain Picard from *Star Trek*." She started embroidering every day to soothe her spirit and help her think. But following other people's designs got boring. So, Shannon says, "I started stitching things I wanted to think about." For example, Shannon was concerned about people getting shot. In fact, one day in 2013, Shannon spent a day logging how many times she encountered the word "gun." "It was seventy-two. Seventy-two times I'd said, heard, or read the word 'gun.' Well, no wonder I needed a way to process it. I have no connection to this thing that is a tool for so much rage. I never need to hold a gun. So that night I stitched a gun as a way to connect with this object." That craft project gave Shannon hours of time to think about a gun outside of the context of the news. To really think about its shape and how it fits into a pocket. How it enables violence. "I realized the power of fusing my two worlds: my activist world and the stitching."

STITCHING MORE GUNS

Shannon's first embroidered gun led to more and more. "I stitched the gun and posted it," says Shannon, "then people asked me to turn it into a pattern, so I did. And then people started making them and tagging me."

Then, a couple weeks after Shannon posted her gun pattern, "I was asleep and a bullet came through my bedroom window. It was beyond loud," Shannon remembers. "It was terrifying to wake up to that sound. I went over to the window, looked outside. There was a moment of 'Have I invited this in? Have I deepened my connection to this thing I don't want to be connected to?' And I had."

Meantime, stitchers were tagging Shannon on their embroidered guns. "There were so many that I said, 'Will you send them to me?' I didn't know what to do with them. And realized I had to turn this into something bigger." And she did. Shannon called for other craftivists to embroider and send gun images. "Within three months, I had 250 guns. They were gorgeous! So then it was like, 'I actually have to do this now.'"

Shannon wanted to use the collection of embroidered art to help fight gun violence. She partnered with Project FIRE (Fearless Initiative for Recovery and Empowerment), which teaches glassblowing to youth in Chicago who have experienced gun violence. "When I teamed up with Project FIRE," recalls Shannon, "they were glassblowers but they said, 'If we're going to do this together, we need to learn how to stitch.' And I

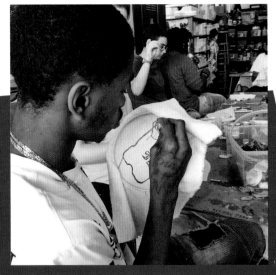

Stitching guns to raise awareness and money. "It's like drawing with needle and thread," says Shannon.

was ready to go in there and sell the idea of embroidery to a bunch of young guys. I said, 'It's like drawing with needle and thread.' And they were like, 'This is dope.' They had no judgment. They loved it. If anything, *I* had assumptions based on gender."

Shannon's End Gun Violence embroidery project grew into a whole craftivist art exhibit in a Chicago art gallery. "It was amazing. We sold everything in the show. We raised over five thousand dollars, and funded the next semester of Project FIRE."

HELPING WOMEN MAKE HERSTORY

Shannon owns two antique cross-stitched pieces embroidered by young girls who signed their names, one by Anna and the other by Molly. Those embroideries got Shannon thinking about who those girls were, and how the stories of their lives would probably remain a mystery. In 2018, Shannon launched a project called Badass Herstory. She put out a call for as many folks of marginalized genders as possible to stitch their stories onto a 12" x 12" square. Or paint or weave or quilt—as long as it's on fabric. Imagine how amazing those squares will look when Shannon displays the stories together as one big Badass Herstory project.

Shannon's Herstory square

A NEW KIND OF SEWING CIRCLE

I tell Shannon that I think the prospect of summing myself up in a square is daunting. Where do I start? "Look, it took me a year to do my own square," she says. But Shannon has become a champ at leading sewing meetups—in person or online—and getting stitchers out of their creative shells. "I have cooked up a pretty solid formula. When we start we *don't* go around the room and say, 'What do you do?' because it creates a hierarchy, like who has the better job. Instead,

I ask for 'name, gender pronoun, and one fun fact.' So when we talk, we talk about 'Wow, you are a champion kite flyer?' We connect in a way that is not based on a power dynamic. Then you start telling your story. It just builds and builds. When women start supporting each other and asking questions, it's magic."

When will the Herstory project be complete? "This is gonna take the rest of my life, I know that. Phase one is lower-hanging fruit, via the internet. Anytime I can get people together and stitch. Phase two is about reaching communities I'm never gonna get into. Places that are isolated. Places of poverty. Can we create kits that other folks get into these communities and capture their stories? The more data you have, the fuller the picture will be." (Go to badasscrossstitch.com for instructions on how to participate.)

RITA'S QUILT

In September 2019, Shannon found an unfinished quilt with hexagonal fabric blocks for each of the fifty states, plus some blocks with big stars, at an estate sale. Shannon could tell that the woman who began the quilt, Rita Smith, was a talented and devoted stitcher. Rita was also a nurse and mom who died at age ninety-nine. Shannon decided to honor Rita's legacy by finishing the quilt. In fact, Shannon wanted to "honor all women crafters and makers whose work has gone largely undervalued throughout time." Think of all the dresses and curtains sewn, all the mending and knitting and quilting done without proper credit or payment or just . . . appreciation. Shannon—who's great at building communities—put out

Shannon (foreground) organized over 100 volunteers to finish and assemble Rita's Quilt.

the call for help with Rita's quilt, and got more than one thousand volunteers. (Way more than she needed—but isn't that great?) Over the next several months, dozens of stitchers from all over the country finished embroidering the blocks, and then more stitchers assembled and quilted them into one gorgeous piece. Many strangers, many hands working together to honor one woman's craftwork—which was a way of honoring all women's craftwork. Rita's Quilt debuted in a Chicago gallery before making a big-deal appearance at the National Quilt Museum in Paducah, Kentucky. Shannon and some of the quilters even got octagonal-quilt-block or needle-and-thread tattoos to commemorate the project, and their time together.

THE ULTIMATE ROAD TRIP

In 2019, Shannon felt like she had the craftivism fire in the belly and wanted to take it on the road, reach out to more stitchers—go on a Badass tour. Giving talks, collecting Herstory squares, and bringing Rita's Quilt to galleries and museums. Shannon says, "The plan was to do everything I did in my free time, but make it my full purpose and focus. Do workshops, create community projects with community and leaders. Art interventions."

Not one to half-ass her plans, Shannon gave notice at her jobs—teaching at a college and also serving as the director of development at a nonprofit organization. Shannon got rid of her apartment, car, and 99 percent of her belongings while she tricked out a cool RV so she and her dogs could hit the road. She scheduled stops and stitch ins all over the country.

THE ULTIMATE PIVOT

And then COVID-19 hit. "I fly to Paducah in March [2020] to be at the National Quilt Museum for Rita's Quilt." Then Shannon got back to Chicago and "We realized COVID was epic and terrible. Everything was canceled, including my fundraiser." Shannon's friends and advisors suggested that maybe she should postpone her tour. "And do what?" was her answer.

In June of 2020, Shannon got into her RV and hit the road "with no plan whatsoever." I ask how that felt. "Terrible and exciting. But I'm a master pivoter. That's what I do. I solve problems." Shannon had to learn how to live a whole new way, how to empty an RV toilet (ick), and how to live socially distanced on campsites or parked in people's driveways. More importantly for her art-activism, Shannon found a new way to be a leader. With a strong digital presence and a not-so-secret love for technology, Shannon made a badass computer command center in the RV. "I figured out how to teach and host these events online. Now it's even better. It's international." I've been to a couple of Shannon's online stitch-ins, where I met crafters from all over the world, from all different time zones. Shannon is building a global network of art-activists.

Since Shannon is mobile, she goes where the weather's warm. She sets up pop-up shows of her work and gives COVID-safe socially distant talks. And she can earn a living teaching college students again, working remotely from her RV.

COVID AS A RESET BUTTON

Even though the COVID-19 pandemic created giant obstacles for Shannon (and the rest of us), it's provided a chance to hit the reset button on our country and culture. Shannon says, "I see this as an incredible opportunity for the whole world to rethink everything, use this as an opportunity for redevelopment. People who refused to see our problems have to face them." Problems like our health care system, racism, poverty, global warming, gun violence.

"I'm worried about our short memory and short attention spans. I hope we don't fall back. I'd rather fall forward." What are some good things we can take away from the pandemic and quarantine? Of course, working from home, working smarter. Shannon also appreciates "the pace with which we are doing things. The epic slowdown." COVID and the quarantine helped us value human connection. "We've seen how supportive people can be of their community. Like cheering for frontline workers." Shannon also appreciates the robust flexibility of the kids in her classes. "When I'm with my students I'm like, 'Young people—dear God, they will save us.'"

DIFFERENT STITCHES FOR DIFFERENT BITCHES

Some craftivists are sweet and subtle. Some are not. "My approach is in-your-face, and I'm an agitator in a lot of ways. Other people just leave something around for other people to find. It's interesting to see all the different ways people do what they do," says Shannon. It's a good reminder that "craftivism" doesn't mean one thing, just like "activism" doesn't mean one thing.

I ask Shannon to suggest a good starter step toward craftivism. Something you can do on your first day. She says, "Make a statement shirt. Stitch something on your jeans or on your bag. Make something public that you are connected to, then go wear it outside and see how that feels."

knitting

Knitting

T-shirts, blankets, sweaters. We touch knit things every day. Knitting is embedded so deeply in our culture, we don't really think about it. So take a moment to think about it now.

Knitting is easy. You can learn the basics in about ten minutes, but it can take a lifetime to master. (I have also heard this about the bass guitar.) Knit fabric is stretchy and flexible, bending and conforming to whatever's near. Knitting is practical. Everyone needs to get warm, so socks and sweaters are always in demand. Knitting is portable. You can knit on a bus or during a lecture. During the 2021 Summer Olympics in Tokyo, Tom Daley, a diver from Great Britain, made news for knitting while watching his teammates from the stands. These qualities—easy, flexible, practical, and portable— helped knitting enter the political arena.

In times of war, our country called on knitters to help soldiers on the cold battlefront. It was a matter of health and safety. Knitting got political and closer to home in 2016 with the Pussyhat Project. Pussyhats helped marchers stay warm and feel unified for a cause.

But here's my favorite thing about knitting: With sewing and quilting, you cut and assemble many pieces of fabric. But a knitter takes one continuous piece of yarn and makes loops inside loops inside loops, row after row, until it forms a hat (or a sock or a scarf or blanket). There's something poetic about following one long piece of yarn on a journey to become something.

Chapter Three

Knitting for Soldiers During WWI and WWII

(1914–1945)

During the world wars, catchy slogans like "knit your bit" inspired civilians to arm themselves with needles and yarn to warm our troops overseas.

EARLY AMERICANS KNIT TO FIGHT THE BRITS

Wartime knitting in our country dates all the way back to the American Revolution. In the 1770s, when we were fighting for independence from England, many merchants and colonists refused to buy luxury textiles like wool stockings from Britain. So colonial American women formed groups to spin local yarn and knit their own damn stockings.

AMERICAN RED CROSS

OUR BOYS NEED SOX KNIT YOUR BIT

World War I poster makes an emotional appeal to women. "Our boys" are the US soldiers.

George Washington and his Continental Army spent the frigid winter of 1779–1780 in Morristown, New Jersey, short of supplies. Washington begged Congress for stockings, shoes, and blankets. There were reports of soldiers barefoot in the snow or with feet wrapped in rags. A woman named Rhoda Farrand of Parsippany, New Jersey, heard about this in a letter from her husband, a soldier. So she rallied hundreds of women in the area to knit stockings for Washington's men.

CIVIL WAR KNITTING

Even after the Revolutionary War ended, friends and relatives would knit for their loved ones in the military. So when the Civil War began, in 1861, the tradition continued. But the Civil War was bigger, bloodier, and lasted longer than expected, so the government started to organize knitting in a more serious way. The North formed the US Sanitary Commission, which tracked the health and needs of Union troops, and called for women to knit blankets and bandages for the wounded. In October 1862, the Sanitary Commission requested, via the *New York Times*, that "the energies of the patriotic ladies of the land be now turned to the knitting of socks and the making of underclothes for the soldier." Groups like the Ladies Army Aid Society in Northhampton, Massachusetts, sprouted up all over the North. They sent their knit goods to the Sanitary Commission for distribution. By the way, members of these volunteer knitting groups were generally white women. Black women formed their own groups, such as the Colored Women's Sanitary Commission in Philadelphia, knitting for both Civil War soldiers and former enslaved people.

In the South, there was less central organization, but nearly every town had some kind of soldiers' aid association. Churches organized war knitting, too. Toward the end of the Civil War, the South was so weakened and resources were so scarce that Southerners sometimes even pulled the wool stuffing out of their mattresses to spin it into yarn. The Civil War ended in 1865, and war knitting slowed to a trickle—temporarily. But in about fifty years, the US would be sending soldiers overseas to fight in World War I. The knitters would be called upon again.

Susan Strawn, professor, knitting scholar, and expert knitter

KNITTING HISTORIAN: SUSAN STRAWN

I've always been charmed by the ads and posters that called for knitters during the World Wars—the old-fashioned fonts, the idea that soft yarn can be a weapon of war. Their appeal to the power of women. But I wanted to know how war knitting actually worked. So I reached out to needlework scholar and expert knitter Susan Strawn.

KNITTING AS A SOURCE OF CALM IN A CRISIS

I assume that war knitting became popular as a source of calm in a crisis, that war knitting helps the knitter as well as the soldiers. Susan agrees. "It's a big factor," she says. "Knitting gives a great deal of comfort. Something about the process of it is comforting. The repetition of the movement."

In fact, this is part of the reason Susan became a knitting historian. She connected to the craft at a young age. "I remember my grandmother teaching me when I was seven. She said that there's something about knitting that put her life back together. After a long, busy day, she would knit in the evening, and somehow things were put back in order and she could go to sleep."

Susan explains, "There's comfort and there's also intellectual stimulation. That's a point that's often overlooked. To knit, you have to be able to understand math and two-and three-dimensional design and shaping and tailoring. You have to know how to correct your errors. You have to understand how to assemble. It is very intellectually demanding. It's not so mindless—it's mind*ful*—you focus because it's intellectually demanding." In this way, knitting is simultaneously calming and invigorating.

WORLD WAR I, THE GREAT WAR

In the early 1900s, there was a buildup of tension among European countries for many reasons—alliances were forming, empires were expanding, and Great Britain and Germany were quietly in an arms race to rule over the sea. But when a Serbian nationalist assassinated Archduke Franz Ferdinand of Austria in 1914, tensions exploded into war. Over the course of the next four years, Russia, Belgium, France, Great Britain, Serbia, Italy, Romania, and Japan (the Allied Powers) teamed up to fight Austria-Hungary, Germany, Bulgaria, and the Ottoman Empire (the Central Powers). The United States tried to stay neutral until the Germans started sinking passenger and merchant ships near England, killing British and American civilians. In 1917, the United States entered the war, joining the Allies.

WWI (then called the Great War) was the first war fought from planes and submarines—previous wars had been fought on land. But there were still thousands of soldiers battling from the trenches. Those trenches were muddy and cold, so keeping hands and feet warm was a constant challenge. There was a serious need for socks and shooting mitts and helmet liners. Time to call in the knitters.

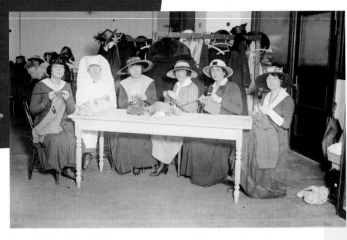

New York City, 1917. Actresses knitting for the Stage Women's War Relief.

CIVILIANS AS SUPPLIERS

I've always thought it odd that the United States government would ask regular people to make supplies for the military. It's like saying, "Oh, we need guns. Can you make us some guns?" I ask Susan about this. "People generally don't know how to make guns, but they knew how to knit. The government was building on a skill that people already had." That makes sense. Plus, Susan reminds me that wool is a renewable resource, and people could provide the wool from their own communities, even their own sheep. Now most of our commercial wool is imported.

SUPPORT GROUP WITH AN HONORABLE CAUSE

With husbands and sons off fighting in WWI, women could get lonely at home. Knitting offered a way to socialize while still serving a cause. If a knitter preferred to be alone or had small children to look after, she could still knit for soldiers on her own, then meet up with a group (kids in tow) to work out her knitting mistakes and questions. But also to connect as people.

SOCIAL NETWORKING, OLD-SCHOOL

Obviously, there was no social media back then, other than newspapers or bulletin boards. So people had to put a little effort into finding ways to connect through knitting. "You might have a friend who can bring you into the fold," explains Susan. "You might contact the Red Cross. Or you'd see an ad for opportunities of where to knit. Could be through your church. A lot of groups were already together, then they took this on."

A detail that warms my craftivist heart: The Red Cross gave out plastic needles that were red, white, and blue. (Though many women used their own needles, which were made of steel or wood.)

SHOOTING MITTS

5-104
PG 10

Soldiers required special mittens that freed up the thumb and forefinger for shooting.

WHAT KNITTERS KNITTED

Once a war knitter volunteered her services, she got her assignment. Susan says, "It could be really simple, like a young girl might be put to work knitting a scarf, made using a simple garter stitch. A more experienced knitter would be knitting sweaters. They always needed socks. They also called for helmets, which were like hoods with a built-in scarf to keep both head and neck warm. And they needed shooting mitts." Shooting mitts? I have never heard those two words together. Susan says, "Shooting mitts were special mittens that freed the thumb and forefinger to operate a gun."

STANDARDS AND QUALITY CONTROL

Making supplies for soldiers was not like knitting Christmas presents. It was a matter of life and death. If shooting mitts were too big, a soldier might have a hard time using his gun. If a soldier's feet were freezing, he couldn't run as fast.

At first people wanted to knit only for their family and friends in the military, but then the government stepped in to set clear quality standards and to oversee distribution. The Red Cross and the Navy League, another government group, got preset knitting patterns out to their knitters. "Patterns were published in magazines that targeted women, like *Women's Home Journal*," explains Susan. "Yarn manufacturers released these patterns, too, because they were savvy enough to know the war wasn't lasting forever, and they were building their market for later."

It may sound like anyone could volunteer to knit for soldiers, but that wasn't always the case. Even in times of great need, some were turned away for ignorant, racist reasons. Susan tells me, "Sometimes a whole Native American reservation was rejected as knitters because officials thought that their knit goods might be dirty or diseased."

KNITTING TO FIGHT PREJUDICE

Knitting bags became fashionable. They were slouchy fabric pouches for carrying needlework along to knit on the go. But knitting bags also served as protection.

"WWI was a time of real xenophobia," Susan explains. ("Xenophobia" means a fear and hatred of people from other countries.) "Anti-immigrant sentiment was just shocking. Anti-German, anti-Italian, anti-Asian prejudice was strong. America was coming off this massive wave of immigration, and they didn't want anyone else from Southern or Eastern Europe." But it helped to show you were a war knitter. "In WWI, if you were a German, if you are part of an ethnic minority and you have your big old knitting bag,

Anytime is knitting time, and a huge knitting bag is a sign of patriotism.

you were much less likely to be seen as a traitor. I see it as protection." I've heard of immigrants today who wear red, white, and blue to avoid harassment. Same idea.

"For WWI in particular, the knitting bag was a sign of patriotism. The bigger the knitting bag, the more patriotic you are. Movie stars had knitting bags. One way to sell fashion is to show knitting bags. It means you're a patriot, and not shallow."

WOMEN KNITTING VS WOMEN VOTING

At the time of WWI, most women could not vote. Some states allowed it, but most did not. And even though women were running households and farms on their own, taking jobs outside the home while men were at war, women were also being asked to knit. It seems empowering, but also patronizing. I ask Susan if she thinks the call for war knitting slowed the progress of women's rights. "Well, there was some evidence that men thought, 'Oh, good, women are back in the home. This is what women should be doing. They're not out marching.'" Susan says, "The suffragists put the vote issue aside and focused on knitting. The women organized along military lines. I think they hoped they were demonstrating their skills at political organization. And they got good media attention for it. I don't think it made a difference in getting the vote. I think they weren't going to get the vote until they did."

SPEAKING OF HATERS . . .

Some editorials in magazines called the WWI knitters "wool wasters." Meaning, the wool could have been used for commercially made blankets or uniforms for the soldiers. But women put notes into the things they made, enclosing little handwritten letters that lifted soldiers' spirits. Plus, soldiers preferred the homemade socks and found them more comfortable because they didn't have seams like the commercially knit socks. The handmade socks were knit from a pattern that created one long, circular tube.

POST-WWI: WHAT HAPPENED TO THE KNITTERS?

The Great War ended in 1918. What followed was a period of American prosperity with a new emphasis on fun. Ever heard of the Roaring Twenties? The economy was booming, largely due to the industrial manufacturing of products like cars. Leisure time was growing. Women were becoming freer. Women helped our nation so much in WWI that many people—including President Woodrow Wilson—argued that women deserved the same voting power as men. In August of 1920, the Nineteenth Amendment to the Constitution passed, granting women the right to vote.

So what happened to all those dutiful, patriotic knitters? Did they retire their needles? Nope. Susan explains, "The yarn business had to make a transition. People were ready to party. The trend shifted to knitting sweaters because people were participating in sports. Like the old letter sweaters people had at school. Sweaters had not been popular before, because women in the 1800s were limited in the sports they could do—things like archery and croquet. But after the war, women were bicycling and playing tennis. The knit fashions dovetailed with these activities that women were finally free to do. They had the vote, and they were working more and playing more."

remember
PEARL
HARBOR

PURL
HARDER

N.Y.C. WPA WAR SERVICES

"Purl" is a stitch used in knitting.

FROM HIGH TO LOW, AND READY TO KNIT AGAIN

The twenties stopped roaring when the US stock market crashed in 1929. Panicked investors stopped investing. Regular citizens started spending much less money. Prices fell. Banks collapsed. Businesses tanked. There was also a terrible drought that hurt the farmers. Unemployment rose until almost a quarter of the country was jobless. The Great Depression set in and stayed for about a decade. Knitting went from fun to practical again. Soon the US government would call on knitters to help their soldiers once more.

US ENTERS WWII, KNITTERS CALLED TO ACTION AGAIN

The economy was unstable over in Europe as well, which—along with other factors—helped Adolf Hitler rise to power in Germany. Hitler made deals with the leaders of Japan and Italy to help him on his quest for world domination. Then on September 1, 1939, Germany invaded Poland. Great Britain and France, seeing Hitler as a threat, declared war two days later. World War II began. The United States stayed out of the fray until December 1941, when Japan launched a surprise attack on Pearl Harbor, Hawaii. Over 2,300 soldiers were killed, and the United States declared war on Japan the next day.

Our soldiers overseas needed socks and shooting mitts once again. And American knitters answered the call.

THE SALES PITCH

I ask historian Susan Strawn how WWII knitting was marketed to women who were in a different place in our culture than they'd been a few decades earlier. Susan says, "One thing I noticed about WWII is all these images I saw in advertising. Ads for shampoo, food, anything. There would be a young woman knitting with a little girl nearby, and she's a clone of the mother. So that's a mother with a husband who's away. That mother in the ads is Penelope, from the myth." Refresher course in mythology: Penelope weaves by day and then unravels her weaving at night, keeping suitors at bay, waiting for her husband, Odysseus, to come home from the Trojan War. She's a good and loyal wife. "She would marry [again] when her weaving was finished. She's supporting a child at home. This depiction of a woman knitting, well, of course it's patriotic to be knitting and to be seen knitting. She's supporting the war effort."

During WWII, the US government put out posters with clean designs and blocky fonts calling for knitting with slogans like "Remember Pearl Harbor, Purl Harder." The WWII campaign for war knitting seems a little louder, a little more spirited than the one from WWI. Susan agrees that during WWII, "the call is more evident. In posters, in ads, everywhere. There was a knitting craze. It was even in popular songs." Songs like "Since Kitten's Knittin' Mittens (for the Army)" and "Knit One Purl Two." (Now look at the song titles playing on your smartphone. A little different, yes?)

KEEPING TRACK

Knitting for soldiers meant counting and tracking what was knit, and using that count to get people fired up for the cause. Kind of like an early reality show. Susan remembers, "When I was a girl, the Oak Park, Illinois, newspaper would publish how many sweaters were made, how many hats were made. Documenting accomplishments and showing it off."

NOT JUST FOR LADIES

In WWII, women really stepped up and took jobs that men left vacant—like in the classic Rosie the Riveter "We Can Do It!" poster. But there were still some men back at home, older men or men doing essential jobs that prevented them from being drafted into service, like firemen. I ask Susan if men "knit their bit," too. "I have talked with men who knit during the war. If a man was at home for some reason and there were women around to show him how, he would knit. I think men like to knit." I wonder if male knitters were teased for doing what was generally considered women's work. "Sure, 'manly' men might make fun of them. But the men who knit were generally proud of what they could do."

ENDING THE WAR

By 1945, the Germans could no longer fight off the Allied forces coming from the west and the Russians coming from the east. The Germans surrendered unconditionally. While the war ended in Europe, it continued in the Pacific as the Allies fought Japan. The battles on the Pacific Islands were bloody, and the US wanted a way to end the war quickly. Scientists had just tested the first atomic weapons. In July 1945, President Harry Truman authorized the use of these weapons. Within weeks, America dropped atomic bombs on the Japanese cities of Hiroshima and Nagasaki—killing well over one hundred thousand people. Japan surrendered. Ragged, tired, but victorious, our soldiers came home.

THEN COMES COLOR

All the war knitting was done in neutral colors, like gray or cream or khaki. So guess what knitters did after the war? Susan says, "They were excited to use color and pattern and texture in knitting. Manufacturers started cranking out patterns. Books, magazines, and department stores encouraged knitting as a social activity." Department stores started selling yarn in more fun, vibrant colors.

CHARITY KNITTING TODAY

Susan tells me about ways to knit for others today—not just for soldiers. "There's knitting for oncology caps. Knitting for people who are homeless, or for transitioning populations. A lot of churches are behind this now. I know a pastor who asked his congregation to knit, then held a blessing of the scarves. You can knit baby layettes for people [in need]. It's acknowledging the economic divide that's now in our country. Sometimes you can start by asking at your local yarn shop how to get involved."

KNITTING FOR SOLDIERS NOW

We still have soldiers stationed all over the world, and you can still knit items to keep them warm and make them feel appreciated. Susan tells me about a knit shop that was sponsoring a charity to make helmet liners for soldiers stationed in cold climates. Susan says, "The helmet liners they are knitting today are almost identical to what was knit before."

Resources:

- **AMERICAN RED CROSS:** redcross.org then search "knit your bit"

- **WARMTH FOR WARRIORS:** warmthforwarriors.com

Chapter Four

Pussyhat Project

(2016–present)

In response to the 2016 election, feminists whipped out their knitting needles to make a new uniform for their protest march. (I was one of them.)

HISTORY MEETS KNIT-STORY

On January 20, 2017, Donald J. Trump was inaugurated as president of the United States. On January 21, 2017, millions of protestors all over the world responded to that inauguration with a gathering of their own. They marched against Trump's election and for women's rights and civil rights of all kinds. Over 470,000 marchers came out in Washington, DC, alone. Between three and five million people marched throughout the US—which is over 1 percent of the population at the time. By the end of that day, there were an estimated five million marchers worldwide, in over eighty countries and on every continent, including Antarctica. Huge numbers of these marchers wore hand-knit Pussyhats. In pictures on all the news outlets, the high overhead shots showed rivers and oceans of pink knit hats with pointy ears. Here's how the hats came to be.

A sea of hand-knit pink Pussyhats helped unify the look and spirit of the 2017 Women's March.

PRE-PUSSYHAT POLITICAL CLIMATE

2016 was a wild election year. The economy was strong under President Barack Obama, who was nearing the end of his second term. The Democratic nominee for president was Secretary of State Hillary Clinton. As an experienced lawyer, former First Lady, former US senator, and acting secretary of state, she was extremely qualified for the job. The polls showed her in the lead, and likely to win. Our country had never elected a woman president and many—including me—thought it was time to have one. Meanwhile, Republicans nominated Donald Trump as their candidate. Trump had never held public office. He was known for building lavish hotels and casinos, for owning the Miss Universe pageant, and for his star turn on *The Apprentice*, a reality TV show.

On October 7, 2016, an audio clip from 2005 surfaced. Donald Trump and then-host of *Access Hollywood* Billy Bush were caught on a hot microphone talking about women. Trump said, "When you're a star . . . You can do anything . . . Grab 'em by the pussy. You can do anything." Many Americans thought Trump's run for office was over. Killed by scandal. But a month later, our country elected Donald Trump to be the forty-fifth president. Hillary Clinton got almost three million more votes than Trump, but in this country we award the office to the candidate with the most Electoral College delegates. Trump won swing states of Wisconsin, Michigan, and Pennsylvania, so he won the overall election, despite losing the popular vote. (Al Gore also won the popular vote, but not the Electoral College, in 2000. The system needs repair.)

So many women were angry that a solid female candidate had lost to an inexperienced man who calls women "dogs," said things on TV like, "If Ivanka weren't my daughter, perhaps I'd be dating her," and bragged about crotch grabbing. Plus, Trump's anti-immigration speeches at his campaign rallies angered many. He promised to build a wall between the US and Mexico. Trump spoke out against people from Muslim countries. Uneasy about the presidency to come, some people took the time between election day and inauguration day to get organized.

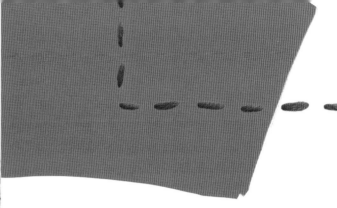

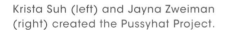

Krista Suh (left) and Jayna Zweiman
(right) created the Pussyhat Project.

TURNING ANGER
INTO CRAFTIVISM

How did so many handmade hats make it to the Women's March that day? Artist and architect Jayna Zweiman and her screenwriter friend Krista Suh organized a worldwide movement that inspired thousands of knitters to make and wear the pink pointy-eared hats. The idea caught on like craft wildfire. I spoke to Jayna to find out more.

BEFORE SHE WAS
A CRAFTIVISTA

Jayna studied economics and visual arts and has a master's degree in architecture. Jayna tells me, "I love how architecture can be an approach to solving societal problems big and small while also acting as a vehicle to bring beauty into the world."

Following graduate school, Jayna was a game designer for a mobile urban scavenger hunt. "I worked on moving people through urban public spaces and experiences, making use of social networking and the relationship between real physical space and virtual space." She was inventing creative ways to bring people together and keep them engaged. Jayna thought a lot about "how to make spaces truly democratic for people. In everything I do, I ask 'How do I make the world better?'"

CRAFTING TO HEAL

In 2013, Jayna experienced a life-altering head-and-neck injury. After three years of rehab, she was looking for a soothing activity to help with her recovery, so she turned to knitting. Jayna recruited Krista Suh to join her. "Krista was the ex-girlfriend of my husband's friend. We became crochet partners at a knitting store I discovered from a Groupon." That store was The Little Knittery in Los Angeles, near Jayna's house. After crocheting and knitting and talking with other knitters, Krista and Jayna realized they shared a passion for feminism and world betterment. Plus, Jayna recalls, "We discovered a community of women who are transgenerational. And every time I sat and knit with them, I learned something."

HOW A HAT WAS BORN

The day after Trump won the election, Jayna knew where to go. "On November 9, I went into The Little Knittery to process, to learn from women who know much more." That same day, talk started on Facebook and other social media about the need for a women's march. Talk turned into organizing a multicity, multicountry march scheduled for the day after Trump's inauguration.

Jayna remembers, "The Women's March was announced and Krista was gonna go." And go big. "Krista was like, 'I'm gonna be naked or make a hat.'" The more they thought about it—and, hey, nudity can be powerful—the more they loved the idea of making a hat. They thought the idea might even catch on. It was something people could actually *do* with their frustration. It was something they could wear and show to connect to other people who shared this feeling.

"We texted Kat Coyle [who runs The Little Knittery], and she designed the hat. We wanted something that did not need circular needles, something easy to diagram. Kat ran with it, and made a pussycat hat. It's a hat style that children have worn, with the

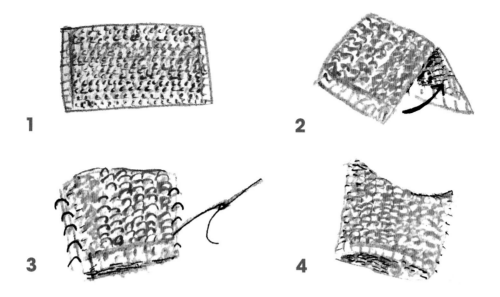

Pussyhat pattern: knit a rectangle,
fold it in half, and sew the sides.

cute pointy ears." But in this new political moment, it had new meaning. "We definitely wanted to reference Trump's 'Grab 'em by the pussy,'" a statement that degrades and objectifies women, a statement that condones sexual assault. Pussyhats take back the P-word, and use it to show strength.

Jayna's architect-urban-space brain was at work, too. "The pink Pussyhat was dual purposed," she explains. "First, to create a big visual splash for the overhead view of the marches. Like the drone view of the AIDS Quilt. Individuals adding up to this huge visual collective. Second, Pussyhats allowed anyone anywhere to take part in this march and be physically represented." People who could not march—like Jayna, who was still rehabbing from her injuries—could knit hats for others and contribute in a real and visible way. Instead of money, people could give their time and their handiwork.

Jayna points out wisely, "The Pussyhat is designed to be easier to make than a scarf, opening up knitting to an entirely new group of people."

IN THE PINK: A CONTROVERSY

Pussyhats were designed to stir controversy and conversation. And they did. Some critics complained that if a Pussyhat is supposed to *be* a pussy (slang for "vagina" or "vulva"), then it does not represent all skin colors. But Jayna explains, "Not all pussies are pink, not all women have pussies. The hat was meant to be a play on words—not an actual body part."

So then why are the hats pink—since they are not meant to represent vaginas? "The hats are pink because that's the color assigned to girls before they are born. We took the color pink and turned it on its head. It's not soft and cute and sweet. Now it's strong. We wanted to take the most feminine color and make its power shine."

And are Pussyhats just for women? Jayna tells me, "Pussyhats are for women's rights supporters. It doesn't matter where they fall along the gender spectrum."

CATCHING ON

Did Jayna expect their Pussyhat idea to catch on as it did, not just across California or over America, but around the world? "Well, I'm an architect. I love scale. This project was designed to become gigantic, but of course I was still surprised. People I hadn't heard from in decades reached out to me about it. The feeling of camaraderie came from everywhere, hearing how it resonated with people."

There were early signs that this thing was going to be big. Trump's victory was declared on November 9, and by Thanksgiving, Jayna and Krista had launched a website with their manifesto and simple knitting instructions. A few days later, Jayna was in New York City for a Pussyhat knit-along, where she "met people who were delightfully obsessed with the idea."

Looking back on it now, Jayna observes, "The Pussyhat went viral because it was well designed, had heart, and the timing was right. Even a brilliant idea won't catch on if the timing is off."

This seemingly simple hat project brought people together for a few different reasons. First, there was the soothing and calming effect of knitting at a time when so many people were so angry and worked up. Plus the satisfaction of making an object you can hold in your hands—and then wear on your head. "It felt like there was a new wave of appreciation for handcrafts and women's work," says Jayna. "Older women, well, it gave them a spark because they were participating in something important and positive." And younger women could get political, too. "My little twelve-year-old cousin was mad that Hillary lost, and taught herself how to knit."

GATHERING STEAM

Since you can knit a hat in a couple of hours, it's easy to make and share Pussyhats. "You make one and you bring it with you and give it to a friend," says Jayna. "You make one and bring it to a yarn store."

Between November 2016 and January 2017, yarn stores across the country started to sell out of their pink yarn. Knitting shops also became a network of distribution points where people could donate and pick up Pussyhats as needed. That is some serious grassroots activity. I ask Jayna how they organized it. Jayna tells me that they gave local yarn stores a simple checklist explaining how to participate. The Pussyhat Project website then listed the local yarn stores, and "this quickly became over 150 different nodes of communication about the project. One of our requests is that they display a Pussyhat and our manifesto. Pussyhat has the word 'pussy' in it. It's hard to forget."

New and old media worked in concert to create a wider reach. They reinforced one another. Jayna remembers, "Our online community drew local news, and local news helped share the project. Then, national news coverage burst on the scene. We had less than sixty days, and we needed to share the idea with as many people as we could!"

KEEPING IT PERSONAL

But to keep things human—even among strangers—Jayna and Krista encouraged knitters to add a note to their hats about why they made it, and what women's issues were important to them. "It was an opportunity to feel seen and heard."

As people across the nation started making and receiving Pussyhats, these pink toppers became kind of a shorthand signal from one women's rights supporter to another. People in Pussyhats would see each other on the street or in airplanes, and they'd nod knowingly. I noticed this when traveling to Washington, DC, to join the Women's March. A lot of travelers were wearing Pussyhats, and it was like we were all on the same team.

THE DAY OF THE WOMEN'S MARCH: LOS ANGELES

"I was in LA watching the rest of the world turning pink," says Jayna. Their vision and passion and hard work were all coming to life, on a huge scale. "It was amazing. We had a physical manifestation of support. We were feeling seen and heard after an election made us feel like we were not seen and heard."

I ask Jayna if there was an oh-my-God moment that stands out from that day. She says, "I think that whole day was an oh-my-God moment. I think starting off with pictures of people flying on planes with Pussyhats. That made it real. Then I thought, 'What if we only have one thousand hats at the march?' We didn't know how many hats there were. There was not a logging process to keep track." But then more and more hats appeared in march after march across the country. And even around the world. Jayna ended up getting a hotel room in downtown LA so she could get the full view of the marchers from above. "It was amazing. There was so much love and support. It felt like it was emanating from the crowd. Everyone was supportive and excited. It was really, really crowded and no one was pissed off."

Fun fact from Jayna, who talked to police officers later: "The cop said it was the nicest group, and people were even picking up litter as they marched."

Me (left) in Pussyhat, college friend Nancy (right), and fellow protestor in full pussy gear

My view as I listened to the speeches

DAY OF THE WOMEN'S MARCH: WASHINGTON, DC

While Jayna was knitting and kvelling in Los Angeles, I was marching in Washington, DC. It felt wonderful to be with strangers, sharing the joy and frustration of that political moment. People climbed trees so they could see everything better and hear the speeches. And so many of us were wearing Pussyhats.

There's a moment I always think about from that day. It was part of the inspiration for this whole book, actually. I was walking in the crowd of proud, excited, amped-up people, when I looked over and saw a marcher wearing a Pussyhat while KNITTING ANOTHER PUSSYHAT! She wore a tool-belt fanny pack that held a spool of pink yarn. She was knitting and walking and maybe even chanting. I was in awe, thinking "Oh hell yeah, that is definitely craftivism!" She was marching for her cause while knitting. And I bet when she finished that hat, she gave it to the nearest hatless marcher, and started casting on stitches for the next hat. It was also a joy to see "women's work" and a "women's march" together in the same eyeful. I wish I'd taken a photo of that knitting marcher. Instead, I took a picture with my dear college friend and a lady I had just met who was wearing a homemade vagina costume.

SUCCESS?

The Pussyhat Project made me proud to be a woman and a knitter and a craftivist. But I ask Jayna—who I know thinks big—if she felt satisfied that day.

"The original goal was to create a sea of pink on the Washington Mall, and we did it," Jayna says. "And everything else was a bonus. The Pussyhat Project has really become everyone's project. Everyone has ownership." Having taken part in the project myself, I had a sense of what she meant, but I ask her to explain. "It laid the ground for us to really talk to each other. It showed our existence as a group, which is part of the cascade of feeling support for each other as humans."

THE AFTERLIFE OF PUSSYHATS

What happened to all those Pussyhats after the first Women's March? "I do still run into people wearing the hats when I've been in Chicago or Boston. Colder places," says Jayna. "I'll wear one when it's cold out here in LA, and I'll get this nod. It's this sisterhood of people for women's rights."

There's a woman on Instagram who took a picture of herself in her Pussyhat every day—even years after the Women's March. She wore her hat in the kitchen and in her yard. There's a photo for every day of the Trump administration. Jayna loves seeing people do stuff like that. "It's really cool that the Pussyhat Project has taken on its own power. This is something you can't predict, and you can't plan. Pussyhats will never be over as long as people are still making them. I still teach people to make them. I think it resonates a lot. Every Women's March since the first one, I stay on the edge and give out Pussyhats. They are free, and people cry. That is the kindest thing: the sense of being cared for by someone you don't even know."

Now there are Pussyhats in museums, like the Victoria and Albert Museum and the British Museum in London, and the Smithsonian Institution in Washington, DC. The hats are there as an example of protest fashion. "It was designed for a moment, but it's finding a place in history," says Jayna proudly.

ART INSPIRATION

I ask Jayna about her influences, especially when thinking up the Pussyhat Project. She says, "Some artworks that really inspired and sparked me were the AIDS Quilt and *The Gates* project." The Pussyhat Project is a natural grandchild of the AIDS Memorial Quilt (see chapter nine). That is, a project where anyone—even people with no experience—can handcraft their own piece of a larger artwork. An art project that gets bigger and more powerful as more and more people pitch in. A project that made a giant visual splash in Washington, DC, and beyond.

The Gates, by Christo and Jeanne-Claude, Central Park 2005, influenced Jayna to think about color on a big scale.

The Gates was created by the artists Christo and Jeanne-Claude, a husband-and-wife team who worked on a grand scale. In 2005, they installed over seven thousand gates in New York's Central Park. Rows of arches hung with bright orange fabric made a river of color that made a splash from above and from the ground.

LESSONS ABOUT ACTIVISM

Even though Jayna has been community-minded her whole career, the Pussyhat Project was her first big activist endeavor, which is always a learning experience. Jayna reflects, "It really brought home the power an individual or a small group can have." She's especially happy that young people got involved. "Teenagers should know they can change the world." Right. You don't need to be voting age to have influence.

"Anyone can be an activist in their own way." Jayna explains, "When people were helping presidential candidates campaign in Las Vegas [in 2016], my friend there was not a US citizen. So he made dinner for the volunteers every night. Instead of hitting the pavement, he nurtured."

After a pause, Jayna adds, "Remember that it's okay to fail." Right—if your craftivist project tanks and nothing changes, you are not any worse off than before. So go ahead and fail. Maybe the next thing will work better. As Jayna puts it, "You never know if you are going to be the person to change things until you try."

Blankets made by hand, each waiting to welcome someone to America

NEXT CRAFT: WELCOME BLANKETS

Building on her experience with the Pussyhat Project, Jayna started her next work of craftivism in 2017: Welcome Blankets for immigrants and refugees. Jayna has been calling for crafters of all kinds and skill levels to make blankets that are 40" x 40" to give to new immigrants as an act of kindness. She explains, "Forty by forty is easy enough to finish, but you still put enough care into it that it hurts a little to give it away."

Once you make a Welcome Blanket, you upload a photo of it, and send it in to Jayna's organization. (See welcomeblanket.org for more information.) Many of the blankets first go to art institutions for display. Groups and piles of these blankets have visual impact, just like groups of pink hats. They illustrate the scale of the problem, but then each blanket later goes to comfort an individual just starting out in this country.

Jayna asks blanket crafters to include notes about their own family history. "My grandparents are all immigrants. My grandfather said, 'I saw the Statue of Liberty and I knew I made it.'" He felt he was getting a fresh start in a country with new possibilities. Jayna wants people to feel welcome like her grandfather did. "It's this incredible opportunity to talk about immigration, and talk about the policies in our country. I see the news every day, and it's nice to be part of making it better." Over five thousand blankets have been made, with more on the way.

With the Welcome Blanket project, Jayna is really playing a long game. "I want to make this a new American tradition. I want a kid today to make a [Welcome] Blanket, then have their kid thirty years from now make a Welcome Blanket. This is my way to create the future I want to see."

Sculpting and Building

Think of how many three-dimensional objects you touch in a day. How are they shaped to serve a purpose? A hairbrush has a handle and bristles, and it tells a story of everyday life. But could it be mistaken for something else? Could it be used for something else? What can a car tire do when it's done being a tire? That sounds like a riddle, but there are practical and beautiful answers.

These art-activists all begin their work with objects we touch and see regularly. They examine the ordinary, and transform it into something extraordinary. Some of their creations are huge—like a zero-waste home. And some fit in your hand—like a memorial sculpture. Some combine shapes and materials in ways no one else ever thought of. Some even make sound. This is beyond recycling. It's rethinking, re-examining. Sometimes for practical purposes and sometimes to provoke emotions. All with the goal of creating a better world.

Chapter Five

Earthships

(1971–present)

Architectural pioneer Mike Reynolds teaches people how easy it is to reduce our carbon footprint to nearly nothing, while still living our best lives.

Earthships heat and cool themselves, while looking like a church or giant jewelry box.

CAPTAIN OF THE EARTHSHIPS

Mike Reynolds graduated from architecture school in 1969. Soon he started questioning how we build houses, and developed a whole new way to do it. He calls his innovative way of building "Biotecture," and the homes he builds are called "Earthships." Earthships are self-sufficient, like a ship on the ocean or in space. They're not connected to any municipal system of plumbing or electricity or gas. According to Mike, they "provide everything a family of four would need. Like contained sewage treatment. Contained heating system. In-house food production [thanks to extensive greenhouses]." Mike's aim is carbon-zero living. With that goal in mind, he works with the forces of nature instead of fighting them. Mike makes the most of the materials and resources at hand. He takes recycling to new heights—and he's been doing it this way long before recycling was a big thing.

HOW IS THIS CRAFTIVISM?

There's no question that Mike Reynolds is an artist. His buildings are beautiful, like giant sculptures that belong on the set of a sci-fi movie. They also serve the immediate community and planet. Mike's Earthships challenge the larger norms. They show city planners a different, more eco-friendly way to run things. Craftivism is for anyone who wants to take part. Because these buildings are low-tech, they are easy to build. Mike teaches people how to do it every day.

HOW TO KEEP YOUR COOL

Based outside of Taos, New Mexico, Mike uses mud to make walls for his houses much like the walls of adobe homes made by the Pueblo Indians. But Mike adds in bottles and cans to make the walls more efficient. He packs tires with sand or dirt to make incredibly strong tire-bricks. The tire-brick walls bear the load of the building while helping to regulate temperature. With the thick walls, solar panels, and smart use of space and airflow, Earthships stay comfortable all year round. "And here in New Mexico," Mike reminds me, "it gets to be 35 below in winter and 109 in summer." All this without using electric heat, fossil fuels, or burning wood.

Tires get a new life, packed with sand and stacked to make sturdy temperature-regulating walls.

GOOD TO THE LAST DROP

Most of us use water once and then send it down the drain. Earthships recycle water four times. They catch rain and snowmelt with aqueducts and store this water in cisterns. The captured water is filtered and then used for cooking and showering. After that, the post-shower water is collected and used to hydrate the indoor garden. Whatever water is left is then used for filling up a toilet. After flushing, Earthship water flows out to collect in a specially designed "botanical cell," which then feeds the landscape. Mike says, "Every building is like an Amazon jungle that produces food, cleans sewage, and also produces oxygen. Landscaping is part of the sewerage system, and it attracts wildlife." The Earthship is a small ecosystem that works with people, and people work with it.

Earthship interior: beautifully sustainable

MIKE REYNOLDS: PRACTICAL DREAMER

I learned about Mike's work from the 2007 documentary *Garbage Warrior*. I fell in love with his beautiful houses, and started down an internet rabbit hole looking to buy one of his homes to retire in someday (a little soon for this plan, but fun to window-shop). Clearly, I wanted to know more. So I arranged an interview. Mike picked up my call as he drove his car in New Mexico, a car which runs on restaurant oil and is patched with pieces of metal from old ovens and washing machines. I picture him driving through the desert like a modern-day Mad Max.

Mike Reynolds also drives a car that runs on vegetable oil.

ORIGIN STORY

As with any superhero, I had to start with the Earthship builder's origin tale. Mike explains, "It wasn't an idea that happened all at once. Back in 1970, I saw a TV newscast with Walter Cronkite [a serious network anchorman]. It said they are clear-cutting timber for houses, and in the future we're going to have a tree shortage. And we're gonna have an oxygen problem and an erosion problem. Then I saw a Charles Kuralt report [a journalist who covered smaller, down-home stories for the national news] on beer cans in our parks. Both of those things together made me go, 'We want to get rid of beer cans and help trees. Let's build with cans.' People said, 'You're crazy using garbage to build with. You are a disgrace to architecture.' But I went ahead and built a demo house that's still standing."

Decades later, the garbage crisis is still a crisis. But Mike Reynolds is making lemonade out of lemons. Or actually, houses out of garbage. "Cans, bottles, tires. You can fill tires with sand to build walls. And if you store mass in the build, it's easier to maintain a steady temperature and save fossil fuel. I lived through the energy crisis. They say the next world wars will be fought over water, and I'm finding a way to live off rainwater. Over the years, I'm responding to what the media says our problem is. And I'm trying to address those needs."

ENERGY CRISIS 101

In the early 1970s, gas and oil seemed cheap and plentiful, and Americans burned it up without much thought. But in 1973, an alliance of Arab countries basically stopped selling fossil fuel to the US, after we took Israel's side in a war. As a result, there wasn't enough gas to satisfy the demand in America. What gas there was became more expensive, and there were long lines at gas stations all over the country. American politicians started to look seriously at ways to reduce fossil fuel consumption. The embargo from the Middle East made the winter of 1973–4 stressful for anyone driving a car or heating a house. The embargo was lifted in March of 1974. For many, that crisis marked the start of the environmental movement. But Mike Reynolds was already on the case.

SIX ESSENTIALS FOR HUMANITY

To Mike Reynolds, a house is not just a cute place to hang your coat and make your bed. It's a functioning system that helps us live. Mike explains, "Humanity needs six things. Every tribe needs six things." And they are:

1. Shelter that doesn't use fossil fuels
2. Electricity
3. Water that comes from the sky
4. Sewerage: Mike adds, "Contained on-site sewage treatment. No municipality does it well."
5. A plan for garbage: "Garbage needs a second use, the way leaves fall from the trees and become dirt."
6. Food

"All these must be built into your living vessel," says Mike. And on Earthships, they are.

FORM VS FUNCTION

Mike Reynolds' Earthships are colorful and have curved walls and swooping lines, like giant jewelry boxes. But does Mike consider himself an artist or, more specifically, a sculptor? "I wouldn't care what an Earthship looked like until it works. What good is a beautiful ship if it sinks? I did make sculpture and art when I was in school. But I want it to be a working machine first and a piece of sculpture second."

EARTHSHIPS ALL OVER THE EARTH

Mike makes sure that regular people can learn how to build Earthships. His organization has internships and workshops year-round, "with students from age twenty-two to sixty. We are trying to put it out there that you can do this. It's a community thing."

And if the community is in crisis, the Earthship team can help rebuild. They've done this over and over in places that have endured disasters. In 2017, after Hurricane Maria ripped through Puerto Rico, Mike mobilized. "We take our crew of ten, and we advertise that we are [rebuilding], so people from all over the world come and help in Puerto Rico. Plus some people on the team are local, Puerto Rican. People are donating that land. We build a house and give it to them. We just give the house away. We are teaching them how to do it and they teach others. We are making a pathway for people to get on and go in this direction." In Puerto Rico, after their Earthship training, people could literally build new houses out of the rubble.

When building an Earthship, bottles and cans take up space so less cement can be used. They also let the light shine through.

"YOU CANNOT ARGUE WITH THE SUN AND THE RAIN AND GRAVITY"

Mike explains, "I'm creating a way to live on this planet. I don't want sustenance to depend on politics or the economy. I want people to be in direct tune with the phenomena of the planet. You cannot argue with the sun and the rain and gravity. These are logical physical truths. I'm trying to help people with a road map to survival." Mike's got a clear set of goals, and he works every day to achieve them.

DIGGING INTO THE LEGAL SIDE OF BUILDING

In the early 2000s, Mike's Earthship building projects were shut down in New Mexico because his structures didn't meet standards of local building codes. His ways of organizing sewerage and heat and electricity were so different from traditional houses that it was like being penalized for speaking another language. So what did Mike do? He bought a suit at a thrift store (always the recycler) and helped propose a new law. "I started out ignoring the law and got in trouble, and then I broke the law and the law won. Then I tried to join them and work with the legislature. It took a lot of energy. It took four years, and the governor signed [the bill]." New Mexico's Sustainable Development Testing Site Act passed in 2007, and opened up the building codes to allow for more experimental housing. (The film *Garbage Warrior* is largely about this chapter in Mike's career.)

HOW TO KEEP GOING

Mike's unconventional ways have meant hitting obstacles and getting frustrated. But he seems to power through. I ask him what helps him to show up on the building site or in his classroom when he feels worn down. He laughs, "Sleep, food, and margaritas. Also, I believe in this so much that it's fun. It's my spiritual thing, it's my exercise, it's my everything. In the morning I can't wait to get up and go to work."

People spend their whole lives looking for something—a job, a quest—that makes them feel that way. Mike says, "It is a gift to find what you like to do, and it takes care of you. I think of musicians I know who get tired of playing a certain song, but they have to pay the bills. I don't get sick of singing the same song, because the song is always evolving. We have really just scratched the surface of what you can do to have human life on this planet, and ways to be an asset to this planet." Even his voice sounds happy and proud as he rolls down the desert highway in his cooking-oil-fueled car.

HEROES OF ALL KINDS

Mike Reynolds is quickly becoming my new hero, and I wonder who influenced him. "Who are your heroes?" I ask. "Well," says Mike, after thinking a bit, "No one person has ever been that impressive. I would say my answer is—a tree. If I could emulate a tree, I would. It takes what it needs and transforms and gives back. And trees are our oxygen and our life." Then I have to know what his favorite tree is. "I like them all. There are Chinese elms that grow around here. People call them weeds. But they make shade, they make nests for birds. I love them." It's not lost on me that he chooses an underrated scruffy outcast tree that gets the job done.

But, for the sake of argument, I push Mike to pick a human being he admires. "If I'm choosing a person, I do land on [Old Testament] Noah, as far as someone I can relate to. He saw the clouds on the horizon. He was on a desert and he built a boat. People called me an idiot and a disgrace when I saw tires as indigenous to the planet and we want to get rid of them. But I'm building something to help people survive." Noah built a ship, and Mike builds Earthships. Both were designed to take us into a new and better world.

WHERE TO START?

It can be overwhelming to think about the state of our Earth, with climate change putting it in crisis, with our culture wasting resources. You might wonder where to start, or how you can make a change. Mike advises, "Just start by understanding those six points, and try to apply them to your life by direct means. Use your garbage. Your toilet water goes somewhere and you need to know where it goes. Get an education."

Or scale up and join a larger community. Take on larger housing projects. Mike invites everyone, "Come build an Earthship. We have an academy. Most people, after they do it for a month with us, they don't want to go back to what their life was. They are getting a glimpse of what is spiritual and logical."

Chapter Six
Border Cantos
(2014–present)

Artist and composer Guillermo Galindo collects objects left behind at the US-Mexico border and sculpts them into sonic devices that sing a new song.

Guillermo Galindo transforms everyday objects into sonic devices, which get a new life in his concerts.

THE POWER OF EVERYDAY THINGS

Everyday possessions can feel like they hold the spirit of the person who owns them. "Think about when a friend leaves a hat or a scarf at your house. It's like you have a piece of them," says Guillermo Galindo. That's why I love to wear my boyfriend's hoodie or my grandfather's high school ring. It's a way of keeping that person near me.

Guillermo wants to honor the possessions and lives of people he has never met: immigrants who have left their things behind at the US-Mexico border. Maybe they buried precious letters with hopes of coming back to get them. Or, more often, they lightened their load before a desert crossing. Guillermo finds clothes, soccer balls, water bottles, inner tubes ("for getting across the Rio Grande," he says), and sculpts them into pieces that make powerful music. Guillermo calls them "'sonic devices,' since they have a completely different meaning and conception than Western musical instruments." Language is important and Guillermo uses it carefully. Border Cantos is the name of this ongoing project. Cantos means "songs" in Spanish—or more literally—"chants," which is a good word for political causes.

BACKSTORY OF THE BORDER

The border between the US and Mexico was first drawn in 1848 to end the Mexican-American War. (A war mainly fought over who got to keep Texas. America won.) For years, huge stretches of the border were just dirt or desert, occasionally marked by marble posts. There was no fence until 1911, when American farmers wanted to keep out stray Mexican animals that might have ticks. The government thought the new border fence might be useful to customs officials who were tracking people and goods crossing back and forth. But the border, which stretches almost two thousand miles from the Pacific Ocean to the Rio Grande to the Gulf of Mexico, took on new meaning and form in this century.

A segment of steel-and-concrete fence along the US-Mexico border

WHEN A FENCE IS MORE LIKE A WALL

In 2006, President George W. Bush signed the Secure Fence Act, which was a plan to build almost seven hundred miles of steel-and-concrete fence to help Border Patrol agents keep out migrants and illegal drugs. There was also an increase in Border Patrol agents, checkpoints, drones, and other forms of surveillance technology. Part of the idea was to block the border where crossing was easier, and steer people to harsher parts—the hottest, emptiest deserts. So yes, the number of migrants decreased, but the crossing also became more dangerous. And more people died.

In 2010, President Obama's Department of Homeland Security froze construction of the fence, but border crossings continued to be dangerous and deadly. Border Control agents were accused of racial profiling and human rights violations. In 2012, the Border Patrol recorded 463 migrant deaths—mostly from desert exposure. And that number has increased every year since.

In 2016, Donald Trump campaigned on the promise to "build the wall." He wanted to add to the existing US-Mexico border wall. He even said that Mexico should pay the construction cost. Once elected, Trump had a hard time getting the US Congress to approve funds for his extensive wall plans. So he made the rules for border crossing stricter. When the COVID-19 pandemic struck in early 2020, the Trump administration basically closed the US-Mexico border, citing health hazards. But thousands of people from El Salvador, Honduras, and Guatemala still tried to cross the border every day. Some were arrested, others turned back.

When President Joe Biden took office in 2021, he stopped construction on the border wall and loosened immigration restrictions. Still, thousands of people attempt the border crossing each day. They are often detained or sent back. Some make it through to the US to start new lives. Hard lives, for sure.

TURNING PAIN AND LOSS INTO ART

When immigration and border conflicts are in the news, the issue can seem big and faceless. But when you see the actual things people had with them as they tried to cross—a shirt or Bible or necklace—you start to see the individuals. Guillermo takes ordinary objects, like a lost shoe, and brings them back to life as art. "I use the vehicle of art to connect people to politics and social awareness." He is a composer, musician, sculptor, performance artist, and teacher. All these skills factor into the Border Cantos project.

BRINGING ISSUES TO LIFE

There's a piece Guillermo sculpted called *Zapatófono* (which translates to "shoe that sounds"). He found a shoe along the border, then added a handle and a microphone. By shuffling the shoe in a tray filled with gravel and bones (also found in the desert), Guillermo brings the scene alive, moving the shoe to re-create the sound of an immigrant crossing the sand and dirt. Guillermo's soundscapes are not always melodic in a traditional way, but they are all provocative.

Guillermo invites us to use our eyes and ears to take in these immigration stories. Even just looking at this picture, you can hear the sound in your mind, while you think about where that actual shoe has traveled.

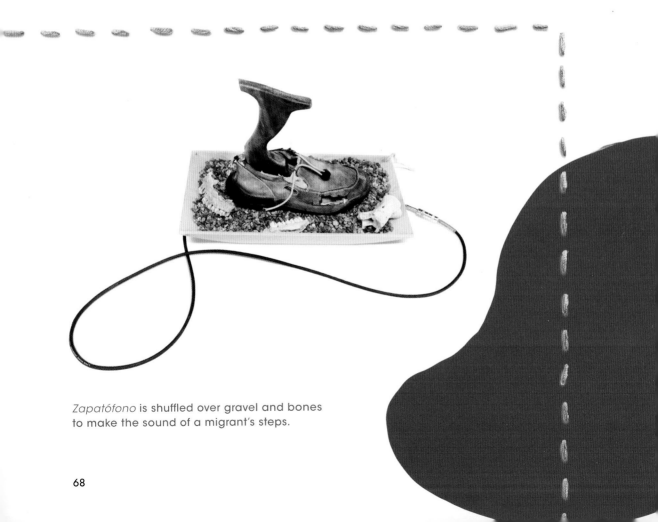

Zapatófono is shuffled over gravel and bones to make the sound of a migrant's steps.

HOW THIS PROJECT STARTED

Guillermo was inspired to make sonic sculptures with found objects after he faced a loss of his own—the death of his father. He explains, "It started around 2006, 2007, when my mother asked me to go through my father's closet after he passed. There's so much of a person in what is left behind." Guillermo was moved by the power of the things he found there and wanted to explore this idea. "I started making objects to heal people around me—artist psycho-magic." He laughs. "I had the basic idea of using personal objects to heal with sound."

Then Guillermo brought this idea to the next level. "Border Cantos began because I was writing a quintet. I was asked to write a piece with a Latin American or Mexican subject. I was using my own objects, making my first pieces from things I found in Laredo [, Texas]. Depending on the geography, you find different things. The first things I found were clothes. People put things in plastic bags and then they cross the Rio Grande."

I ask Guillermo what actual objects stick with him the most. "The toys," he says. "A children's Bible. A *Doctor Zhivago* book translated into Spanish. Personal IDs, letters from relatives." While the work sometimes makes him sad, it also helps him feel that he is creating something new from what others have lost. He is paying tribute to their lives and the things that mattered to them. Says Guillermo, "Thousands of people cross every day. They could be shot—or in a detention center. But I'm giving them life, keeping their stories alive."

INTERNATIONAL INFLUENCE FOR INTERNATIONAL ISSUE

Guillermo Galindo grew up in Mexico City, Mexico, but now lives and works in Oakland, California. Guillermo is influenced by music from all over the world—African percussion, a Japanese stringed koto. When sculpting his sonic devices, Guillermo prefers to "work opposite of the way of Western thinking. In the West, you force material to make the sound you want to hear. I think instead you should listen to the object. Listen to it and make the sound it wants to make."

DIFFERENT OBJECTS TELL DIFFERENT STORIES

Migrants are not the only people who leave things behind along the US-Mexico border. Border Patrol agents work there, too. They leave behind shotgun shell casings, ammunition boxes, chairs, cans with bullet holes from target practice, and water jugs they find in the desert and slice or shoot up so that the water spills out and cannot be saved. You definitely feel the presence of the agents in Border Cantos, just as someone crossing the border feels their presence. For one sonic device, Galindo strung shell casings around a soccer ball, which he shakes for percussion, like an African shekere. He made a CBP (Customs and Border Protection) flashlight into a trumpet. That piece is called *Tonk* for the derogatory nickname some agents allegedly give migrants, as in the sound a flashlight makes hitting a person on the head.

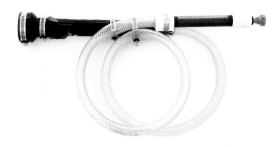

Trumpet made from a border patroller's flashlight

Llantambores (roughly translated, means "flattening drums")

In Guillermo's *Llantambores* sculpture, the skins of the drums are inner tubes used for river crossings, and the frame is a structure that migrants put on their shoes to flatten out their footprints in the sand. The barbed wire is from the border fence.

REACTIONS TO THE WORK

Guillermo's Border Cantos—with accompanying photographs by collaborator Richard Misrach—has been shown in museums to packed crowds. Guillermo has performed concerts with these sonic devices in orchestra halls and universities. His work has reached academics and intellectuals. But I can tell what audience he cares about the most. "In museums, several times I saw the janitors looking at the work. I go to them, 'What do you think?' and they say, 'It reminds me of this or that relative' and 'My family crossed the border.' One security guy at a museum liked the work, so he said, 'Whenever you want to park here, you can park here.'"

Guillermo believes that artists can illustrate political issues—like immigration—in a different way. Different from the journalists and politicians. "Politicians say what they want to get a vote. An artist has language that can explain things in a way that none of those other people can do."

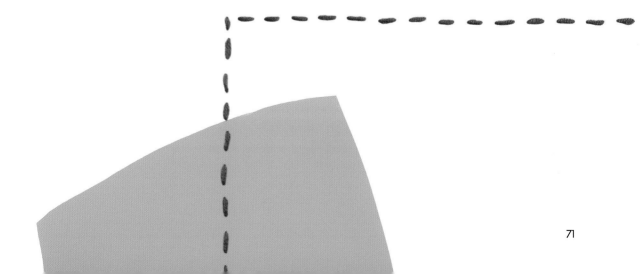

THE ARTIST AS A YOUNG MAN

Guillermo makes art and teaches college in California's Bay Area. He has lived in the US for many years, but he grew up in Mexico City. As a teenager, he recounts, "I was into progressive politics. I was very non-conforming. Always questioning. A rebel with a devious imagination. I also liked reading a lot. I was always interested in culture and language and politics. My family, although they sold pianos, were not very supportive. They'd say, 'He's not into money and fashion.' They were worried about me. I still do the same weird things, but now I get paid."

Growing up, Guillermo found a variety of heroes and sources of inspiration. John Cage, the minimalist composer, and Johann Sebastian Bach, the German Baroque-era composer. Also the psychologist Carl Jung, Joan of Arc, Gandhi, Mother Teresa, and Malcolm X.

STARTING TO LEARN

Sometimes, the hardest part about making art is just starting. I know this from experience. I can plan and gather materials and research for days and weeks, in order to avoid actually cutting fabric or carving a stencil. It's intimidating. What if I mess up? What if I'm terrible at this? I'm completely untrained, so where do I begin? I ask Guillermo if a person needs to be formally trained to make art. "Not necessarily—especially for music. In many traditions, a craft is passed on to generations. A drummer plays the drum and chooses a kid who learns to play. It's also like the tradition of the loom and the textile. There's the tradition of passing the skills and the stories to their daughters and granddaughters." This rings a bell for me because I learned knitting and crochet from my grandmother, but also taught myself what she didn't know. And now there are online videos on how to do anything. And you can hit pause as much as you like and make all the mistakes you want.

Guillermo believes that people could—and should—teach themselves more. "We depend a lot on services. No one repairs things

themselves anymore. In order to make my instruments sturdy, I had to teach myself to make them."

TIME TO ACTIVATE

I ask Guillermo what a good starter project would be. And he suggests a mini version of a healing sculpture/instrument. "Pick up an object that belongs to a person in your family or friend that has a problem. And realize how to make sound out of it. And give it to your friend. Like a hat or bottle of medicine." At first I am baffled by this. I ask, "How does a hat or medicine bottle make a sound?" Guillermo explains you can rub across the texture of a woven hat with your hand to make a quiet, rhythmic sound. A medicine bottle is easy—tap it with your fingers or fill it with some buttons or stones and shake it. "You can explore how things sound. There are things you can kick and step on to make sound. Hitting and tapping and stepping on things are also ways to connect to an object. And you become part of the art. You are the activator of the instrument."

That's art: activating an object, giving it life and power.

Chapter Seven
This Is Not a Gun
(2016–present)

So many unarmed people have been shot by police officers who say they saw a gun. But there was no gun. In response, artist Cara Levine is sculpting the objects that the victims actually held.

WHITE LADY ALERT

I grew up in an upper-middle-class Chicago neighborhood, and now I live in New York City, near a nice park. I've never been afraid of the police. In my experience, police officers direct traffic, manage crowds at parades, and maybe give me a speeding ticket. But the sight of a police officer in my rearview does not make me fear for my life—and that is white privilege.

Hairbrush for Khiel Coppin, 56 Carving Hours

It took me a long time (too long) to realize how police encounters can be so different for people of color. In 2018, I was working on a TV talk show with a Black host. In a meeting, he joked about what officers say when they stop and search you. Like, "I hope you don't have anything sharp in your pockets." I was surprised that he had this police-search patter down because he'd been through it so many times. Everyone Black in the room laughed. An "Oh God, I know," laugh, because they'd been stopped, too (or their siblings, friends, sons, or daughters had). I was shocked that this was anyone's normal.

GEORGE FLOYD AND BLACK LIVES MATTER PROTESTS

On May 25, 2020, in Minneapolis, Minnesota, an unarmed Black man named George Floyd was handcuffed and pinned facedown on the ground while Derek Chauvin, a white police officer, held a knee on George Floyd's neck for more than nine minutes. A crowd watched, some begging Chauvin to stop and others taking videos. Three other officers at the scene did not try to stop Chauvin. George Floyd died in plain sight of these officers, the bystanders, and ultimately the entire world. Floyd was accused of trying to pay in a store using a fake twenty dollar bill. Floyd didn't get a trial. He certainly didn't deserve a death sentence.

The next day, people in Minneapolis gathered to protest George Floyd's death. This combination of 1) growing numbers of unarmed Black people dying at the hands of police, 2) the COVID-19 pandemic crisis causing high unemployment and general anxiety, 3) this act of police brutality on video for all to see—these three factors were sparks that caught fire. And that fire spread across the country and beyond.

There was already an organized movement called Black Lives Matter (BLM), started in 2013 by three women— Alicia Garza, Patrisse Cullors, and Opal Tometi—in response to the death of Trayvon Martin and the acquittal of his killer (see page 119). For years, BLM had been organizing peaceful protests against police brutality. In June and July 2020, people of all colors put on masks for COVID safety and joined BLM protest marches in every major city in the US, and in small towns, too. At least sixty other countries held Black Lives Matter protests. The national and global conversation about police brutality was evolving and getting louder.

Artist Cara Levine at a This Is Not a Gun sculpting workshop in Los Angeles

CARA LEVINE, ART-ACTIVIST

Cara Levine is an accomplished artist and an associate adjunct professor at an art college in Los Angeles. She is also an art-activist. Even before the wave of Black Lives Matter protests of 2020, Cara thought a lot about how people of color are at higher risk for experiencing violence at the hands of the police, and how Black people are killed by the police at about three times the rate of white people. Since 2016, Cara has been organizing an art project and ongoing community action called This Is Not a Gun (TINAG).

There are dozens of objects that police have "mistaken" for a gun in the hand of a Black or brown person: wrench, wallet, cordless drill, Bible, cell phone, hairbrush, and more. Cara has been sculpting these objects, one by one, from wood. And Cara started a series of community workshops where people sculpt those not-a-gun objects from clay.

THE ORIGIN TALE

I ask Cara how This Is Not a Gun began. Was it a light bulb moment or a slow burn? "A little of both," she remembers. "In my art practice, if there's something I don't understand, the act of making helps me investigate what I can't grasp. This was a time in California where people were dying from police shootings." In 2016, according to *The Sacramento Bee*, police in California were killing a suspect "about once every three days." Mostly minorities. In these cases, authorities argued that the person was thought to be "threatening a police officer," which means perceived to be carrying a gun. Even if there was no gun.

Cara recalls, "This list crossed my screen. A list of objects that were 'mistaken' for guns in civilian shootings. But I thought, 'This list is empty. This list is clickbait. Nothing is described here. I need to see these objects.' That was the impulse to start the whole project."

And so she began. Cara used her carving time to listen to books—primarily books on the history of race in the US. "I'm an educated person with a diverse friend group, but I had to understand better. Why are police disproportionately shooting Black men? And pretending to have every reason to do it." Cara made sure to learn about each case, the people involved, and the circumstances.

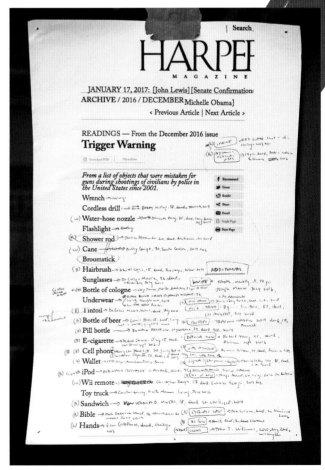

List that set This Is Not a Gun in motion, annotated with Cara's notes

HOW AN OBJECT TELLS A STORY

As the wood becomes a hairbrush, the person who held it comes alive, too. Cara's carvings of everyday objects help you imagine the people who used them. Objects tell stories. When I first interviewed Cara, she was carving the sixteenth object on the list.

"It's a toy truck," she says. "A caregiver for a disabled man was shot. The police thought the disabled man had a gun. He had a toy truck. It's really sad. The caregiver lived. They both lived. People of color *with* a disability are doubly targeted because police aren't prepared to interact with 'otherness.' There is a deaf man on this list who was shot while trying to sign. There's a man with bipolar disorder who tried to shield himself with a Bible."

Toy Truck for Charles Kinsey and Arnaldo Rios Soto, 83 carving hours

ART LEADS TO CONVERSATION

Cara wanted to open the conversation about race and police violence. In 2016, Cara started teaming up with local artists and activists of color to co-lead free workshops where anybody—from high school students to senior citizens—could use clay to sculpt the objects that have been mistaken for guns.

I ask Cara if it was the solitude of the wood carving that led her to open up the project to the community. She explains, "The carving created a lot of time to think and listen. I know that this is not my story. I'm not in danger, but I'm still grieving. Differently and along with many others. That's when I started the workshop as the model for creative community action. I feel it's my social responsibility. I back off as the author and artist. I partner with someone local, and we hold a cross-racial dialogue at each event."

EKA CO-LEADS WITH CARA

Ekaette Ekong teaches yoga in Los Angeles. She's also the founder and editor-in-chief of *Woke* magazine, which covers social justice, wellness, and more. Cara and Eka met years ago when they were both teaching yoga at Coachella, and they have stayed good friends. Cara invites Eka to bring all her warmth and healing skills to co-lead This Is Not a Gun workshops whenever she can—she's done four sessions so far. I talked to Eka about her experience.

MIND AND BODY

At the workshops they facilitate together, Eka and Cara set people up with their clay and ask them to sculpt one of the objects that has been mistaken for a gun. The very act of touching clay relaxes people and helps the walls come down. "Like kids playing in mud," Eka says. "Then we pause. And I lead them in a meditation." Each meditation is different. "I have an outline, based on what just happened the week before, the month before." It's not hard to connect the current news to the stories of This Is Not a Gun.

Ekaette Ekong co-leading a This Is Not a Gun clay workshop in Berkeley, California

   "When I am leading the meditation, it's also for me, because I need to feel safe somewhere. It also gives me a way to be of service because these are things that are not being spoken at all. I ask them to consider the objects. 'What is it that is weaponizing this object? What is that bringing up for you?'"

As participants work with their hands, Eka and Cara guide the discussion. "There are times we have questions on slips of paper on the table, and we'll ask people to read them out loud." The questions are tough ones: *What has your experience been with the police? How would you feel if you were stopped holding this object? How can we begin to change policing?* The questions are jumping-off points for important conversations.

RELATIONSHIP TO POLICE

I ask Eka about her encounters with the police. She grew up in LA, living in an upper-middle-class predominantly white neighborhood. Cops would definitely keep an eye on her—and not in a nice way. "We were one of two Black families, so we'd get the 'Are you in the right place?' kind of questions."

In Los Angeles, driving means the fear of getting pulled over. "My father was pulled over by police many times. He was a physician. One of the first times, he was on the way to an emergency. After that he always had to make sure he had something on him." Some kind of ID that proves he's a doctor. Even today when Eka sees an officer in her rearview mirror: "I am always aware of where they are. I'm always stiffening, keeping my hands on the wheel at ten and two."

SPEAKING FREELY VS CODE SWITCHING

Eka told me about one TINAG workshop she was co-leading. There were about eighty participants, mostly—but not exclusively—people of color. Some younger and some older folks. When Eka and Cara started talking about police violence, the workshoppers of color seemed hesitant to speak freely. Eka recalls, "We said, 'Yeah, I know there are white people here, but you can say what you really want to say.' I think it goes to code-switching." Code-switching, she explains, is when, "as a person of color, you're aware of who you are around, and what you should say. Around your friends you can just say what you want. Speak in vernacular. Whereas with code-switching you have to think, 'Wow if I say this, what are the repercussions going to be? Will I lose my job or upset someone?' We have to police our tone [when speaking with white people] to protect ourselves."

OPENING EYES

I ask Eka if she notices white people realizing the pattern of police violence in this country. She says, "Yes, I hear a lot of 'I had no idea this is happening' and 'Where have I been while this has been happening?' My experience is, this has been going on, but now it's on camera. Now there's a shame of grappling with it." Sometimes people can't sit with the discomfort the topic brings. "Some people have felt hurt in the workshops. Like we talk about racism and they say, 'I don't do that. My family doesn't do that.' It's painful to hold up a mirror to how you are showing up in the world."

TAKING FEELINGS TO THE NEXT PLACE

As the workshop winds down, people finish their clay sculptures. Eka leads the group in a closing meditation and a moment of silence. Then they give their sculptures to Cara and Eka to be fired in the kiln and added to the larger collection of not-a-gun objects.

After everyone goes home, Eka says, "I get down from the adrenaline high. I have to go home and be quiet because someone who looked like me, people that look like me were killed."

ARTISTS ADDING THEIR MARK

In making the object, the sculptor thinks about its shape and what it must have looked and felt like in someone else's hand. Cara says that when she sculpts something from the list, "I just copy it. I try to re-create the object out of clay. But young people add things. Like, they make the glasses and write *How do you see me?* on them. They add names of lives that have been lost."

Object made at a TINAG workshop. Trayvon Martin was carrying a bag of candy when he was shot and killed in 2012.

HOW THE BLM PROTESTS OF 2020 CHANGED THE CONVERSATION

I ask Cara how it feels to be an art-activist on the issue of police violence at a time when many people in America seem to be talking about it. "I still feel like a newcomer," Cara says. "Even though I have been talking about this for five years. I hope that we can see real change. But right now in the news, I learned that the officer who shot Jacob Blake in the back at point-blank range [in August 2020, in Kenosha, Wisconsin,] is not being prosecuted. Blake is paralyzed. So in other ways, I see no change."

But Cara takes a breath and tells me about some good signs, like a new police chief in Richmond, California, who leads with "an emphasis on communication, de-escalation. He works on integrating the police with the community. Police departments all over the country trying to make these changes. It's not brain surgery to see what we need—reallocation to social services."

WHITE ALLYSHIP

Cara recognizes her complicated position as a white woman in this work. She believes that while Black voices should be leading the national discussion of racial equity, "white people also need to be in the conversation." That can get uncomfortable, which is okay and even necessary. "We are all connected by this trauma. To disengage white people from the conversation is a disservice to social justice. White people are profoundly implicated in this history and can be a part of the healing process."

I ask Cara how she feels about the concept of the white savior, or a white person who provides help to non-white people in a self-serving manner. Cara says, "Yes, 'white saviorism' is definitely a thing. As a concept, it goes deep. It's colonialism. It's age-old." White people have been trying to "help" for a long time, so it's against that backdrop that Cara has encountered some skepticism.

Cara explains, "I am the steward of this project. But I have dozens of collaborators—people profoundly invested in race equity through their work. I'm not alone. That is part of [how I combat] this white savior thing. I'm not saying 'Follow me.' I'm saying 'I want people to listen to Black people and Black stories.' I don't want the microphone, I want the conversation to happen."

Cara co-hosts workshops where people sculpt objects mistaken for guns, like this garden hose nozzle.

THIS IS NOT A GUN KEEPS EVOLVING

In 2020, a book edition of the This Is Not a Gun project was published. A diverse group of over forty artists, teachers, poets, and activists contributed. Each wrote about one of the objects mistaken for a gun. "I want it in as many hands as possible," says Cara. "I want it in schools."

WORKSHOPPING IN NEW WAYS AND PLACES

Even with COVID-19 limitations, clay workshops continued. On September 25, 2020, This Is Not a Gun held a socially distant outdoor workshop on City Hall steps in Los Angeles. "We brought some fold-up tables, brought the clay. It was life-giving. They had these street poets there and we read from the book."

THE POWER OF MANY

Collective art projects have extra power, like a choir singing. Cara has gathered the finished, kiln-fired ceramic pieces from over five years of This Is Not a Gun workshops. In November 2020, she laid them all out in the Tiger Strikes Asteroid Gallery in Los Angeles. "They are on a pale blue floor. There are 300 objects. It feels massive. It fills the whole room. It feels like a memorial. People walk in and people get quiet. It felt important to give it some breathing room." These pieces are beautiful, made by many hands, but remind us of those who died unjustly.

Participants working on clay objects at Los Angeles City Hall, 2020

STILL CARVING WOOD

Throughout all this organizing, plus teaching full-time, Cara is still carving wooden objects from her original list of twenty-three things mistaken for guns. I check in with Cara after our initial conversation. "Now I'm on the seventeenth object. A beer bottle. I'm not going in any particular order." Cara says she picks what to carve next based on "practical things like time, like do I have the material to do it," but also more spiritual factors like the shape she feels like making, and the story she feels she can sit with. She explains that as she spends time working on each object: "I'm just overwhelmed by the plainness, the ordinariness. As I carve more, I just recognize more and more its not-gun-ness."

STARTER KIT

I asked Cara to suggest a good starting point for a first-time art-activist. "The first thing I go to is trying to identify the feelings in your body. The biggest feeling that comes up for me in my studio is sadness and grief. Then try creating some representation of those feelings—drawing, dancing, or throwing clay against the wall. Articulating feeling through material." But what's the goal? What's the point of that? "To get it out of you and to show other people. And that's how art becomes a language. It feels good to make something. There was not a thing before, and now there's a thing."

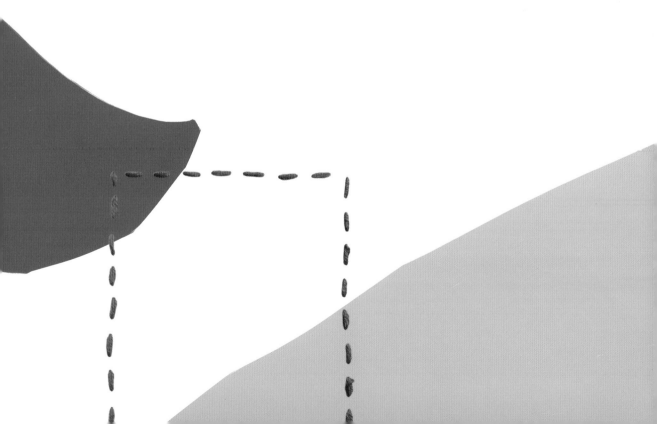

quilting

Quilting

Quilters are no-nonsense doers who have been recycling before recycling was even a word. They are transformers who save smaller bits of fabric to sew up into a greater whole. They are collaborators who make art together. Quilters also have a tradition of documenting history—like making patchwork out of Grandpa's shirts or making a wedding quilt with the date stitched in the middle.

The next three chapters show quilters from different times in American history, documenting their sorrows and dreams, while aiming for a better future. They made quilts to voice their opposition to slavery and quilts to remember those lost to the AIDS virus. And today, there are young people stitching their feelings about racism, poverty, literacy, climate change, and more—often sewing for the first time. As works of craftivism, quilts can do more than warm beds—they can raise money, express love, show anger, and demand action.

Chapter Eight

Quilts and Anti-Slavery Bazaars

(1830s–1850s)

Ladies (and it was mostly ladies) with needles and thread played a real part in raising awareness and money to fight slavery through craft fairs.

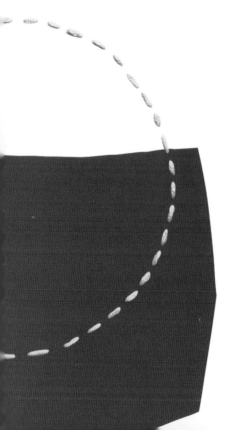

BACKGROUND: SLAVERY IN AMERICA, THE BEGINNINGS

Enslaved people were a part of American history as early as the 1600s. Dutch colonists brought people from African countries, chained in slave ships, to labor in their growing sugar and shipping empire. Other European countries followed suit as they settled into the new colonies, exploiting slave labor to work the land, build buildings, weave fabric, and tend babies. Founding fathers George Washington and Thomas Jefferson owned enslaved people. Apparently, owning human beings while fighting England for the right to "life, liberty and the pursuit of happiness" was not an ethics problem.

After the Revolutionary War, one by one the northern states outlawed slavery (starting with Vermont). But the process was gradual. Cities like Boston and Philadelphia became more industrial, more dependent on machinery. The machinery workers earned wages (low, low wages), but the northern economy did not depend on the labor of enslaved people. By 1804, slavery was illegal throughout the North but still legal in the South. Note: It's tempting to oversimplify this moment as North = Good and South = Bad. But it was easier for the North to let go of slavery because the region was making a lot of money from factories. The South was much more reliant on the labor of enslaved people for their plantations. When morality bumps up against the economy, many choose what's best for the economy. This is still true.

KING COTTON RULES

Eli Whitney's cotton gin

Southern farmers had been growing tobacco relying on the labor of enslaved workers, but that crop was not making money like it used to. The land was good for cotton, but it took hours and hours of work to pick the seeds out of the cotton fluff. The labor was free, but the going was slow. Then in 1794, inventor Eli Whitney patented his cotton gin ("gin" is short for "engine") and changed history. The cotton gin could clean seeds out of fiber-y cotton plants faster than a person ever could. The cotton business boomed, and soon the South provided cotton to most of the world. "King Cotton" they called it. Plantation owners needed workers to farm the ever-expanding fields of cotton. And the labor of Black, enslaved people was their solution.

By the 1830s, tensions were running high between the industrial North and the agricultural South. Philadelphia and Boston were at the center of the growing abolitionist movement (as in, the movement to abolish slavery). Southern farmers felt too financially dependent on the slavery system to give it up. In fact, they were willing to go to war over it. But that came later.

BABY QUILT FOR A GROWN-UP CAUSE

As a quilter, I like to look at antique quilts for inspiration. I find pictures of them in books, on Pinterest, on museum sites. I get lost in the looking the way other people get lost in cookbooks. And if I can learn the story of a quilt, even better. A picture of this cradle quilt led me into a corner of history I'd never heard about. The quilt is neatly pieced in a pattern called Evening Star, and has an abolitionist-themed poem printed in the middle. It was sold at an anti-slavery craft bazaar in 1836. Craftivism in action! I got excited about it and found a scholar who had studied this very quilt. I needed to learn more.

Handmade baby quilt sold in Boston, in 1836, to raise money to fight slavery

MARIAH GRUNER: NEEDLEWORK SCHOLAR

Mariah Gruner is a historian who got her PhD at Boston University. She writes about the political importance of American women's decorative needlework, from 1820 to 1920, when many needles were blazing. Her studies start with the anti-slavery movement and end with women's fight to get the vote. The anti-slavery movement in many ways led to the women's rights movement. The anti-slavery movement was for many women—and we are talking about mostly white women—their first step into political activism.

QUILT WITH A MESSAGE

I ask Mariah about the history of this baby quilt. She says, "The maker was likely a Massachusetts woman named Lydia Maria Child. She wrote stories for children. She was a novelist and a journalist, as well. She was the editor of a weekly newspaper, the *National Anti-Slavery Standard*, for quite some time. So she was deeply involved in institutional anti-slavery work." In the center of the quilt, Lydia wrote out a verse from "Remember the Slave," a longer poem by Eliza Lee Cabot Follen, a prolific writer, "informed by her Christian faith. She was an abolitionist as well," explains Mariah. The verse reads:

Anti-slavery-themed poem in the center of a baby quilt, which was sold at an abolitionist craft fair

> Mother! when around your child
> You clasp your arms in love,
> And when with grateful joy you raise
> Your eyes to God above.—
> Think of the negro mother, when
> Her child is torn away,
> Sold for a little slave,—oh then
> For that poor mother pray!

This is a poem meant to get fair-goers by the heartstrings. It's meant to remind white mothers of what slavery does to Black families. This quilt, an object made for warmth and comfort, features a sharp political message conveyed through craft and through the home. As Mariah points out, "I think people retreat into their homes to *not* confront their political reality. But there isn't a retreat. Everything you buy is related to the political world and these craft items make it explicit." A quilt is something you live with for a while, unlike a newspaper headline you throw away. "Abolitionists believed that spending time with these images changes something about you internally," says Mariah.

OVERTONES OF WHITE SAVIORISM

Clearly, the poem doesn't 100 percent stand the test of time. It's not okay to say "negro" anymore. The verse feels patronizing. The poet is a white artist aiming at a white audience, and casting the white people as the benevolent liberators. "There is absolutely an element of white saviorism to these pieces," says Mariah. "They imagine the pain and suffering of Black people and do that in order to develop themselves as sensitive people, to cultivate and perform their ability to *feel* keenly. That was a real value at the time, a way that you proved how 'civilized' you were." So it's important to note that though pieces like this were made with a real desire for change, there was also a bit of self-congratulation, too. "I don't want to say that this was insincere work at all. It was done at great risk and was sincerely felt. But it was also problematic for its emphasis on the status of Black women as suffering, supplicating subjects waiting to be freed by white activists." Mariah points out, "Many enslaved people liberated themselves. And many Black people were involved in anti-slavery work. The dynamic of white anti-slavery activists imagined as 'the liberators' is troubling."

LADY-POWERED AMERICAN CRAFTIVISM

This baby quilt was for sale in Boston's third annual Anti-Slavery Fair, held in December 1836 and organized by the Boston Female Anti-Slavery Society—or BFASS. There was a women-run political group, even back then? "Yes, women were considered the keepers of the morals in the household," Mariah explains. "Their realm was the domestic space. Women could use the platform of the moral domestic space to object to slavery. It's an interesting blurring of public and private."

Up until that time, it was acceptable for women to form charity groups for causes that were not controversial, like helping poor children who were orphans or raising money for Christian missionary trips. But taking on slavery meant ruffling feathers. Women of the Boston Female Anti-Slavery Society were giving their opinions on matters of economic importance, normally a man's arena. Women were raising money themselves, which gave them power. Women were literally speaking up in public gatherings. Mariah emphasizes, "This was a huge transgression for many. Lots of church leaders wrote that women involved in public antislavery organizing were literally violating divinely ordained 'separate spheres.'"

SEWING CIRCLE AS POLITICAL CIRCLE

Mariah notes that "a lot of the female anti-slavery societies started as anti-slavery sewing circles. But they might just be called 'sewing circles,' where women could gather and no one really questioned why they gathered." Of course. Who on earth is threatened by a bunch of ladies sewing? What could be more harmless than that? In fact, sewing circles were a place for women to exchange news and discuss ideas out of earshot from the men who didn't always approve or agree. "Women read copies of anti-slavery pamphlets or newspapers together while they were stitching."

Sometimes the "sewing circle" would be dropped from a group's name because they simply weren't actually doing much sewing.

"For example," says Mariah, "the Rochester Ladies Anti-Slavery Sewing Society formed in 1851, but ended up dropping the 'Sewing' from their name. They were doing other things. Organizing lectures, raising funds, reading and circulating anti-slavery literature."

WHY CRAFT BAZAARS?

Mariah explained that there were two main reasons the women's groups started the bazaars. First, this was just a straight-out way to raise funds for their cause with the skills that they had. "These fairs became huge moneymaking operations. They were often held before Christmas and did really well." Middle-class women were realizing that quilting and lace-making and embroidery were not just pretty decorations. That their work had a greater value. As Mariah put it, "They were learning the lesson, 'You are going to be paid for your work.'" Until then (and still a struggle now) women were not paid for the work of raising kids, cleaning, cooking, and making pretty things for the home. Women had to get money from their husbands or fathers. But the craft fairs allowed these "pretty things" to make money and serve a greater purpose.

Dr. Mariah Gruner, needlework scholar, working with anti-slavery textiles in Colonial Williamsburg

The other reason for the fairs was more sophisticated. The fairs sold dry goods and other staples people needed. The fairs made an early attempt at ethical shopping. According to Mariah, "It was about trying to purchase goods that have been produced without slave labor. So kind of a boycott and consciousness raising." Shopping fair trade is challenging—both now and then. "Right," says Mariah. "How do you lead a clean life in a dirty system? It was hard to do. At that time, sugar and tobacco and cotton were all grown and made with slave labor." So they helped people shop with a conscience, or at least tried to raise awareness. Mariah says, "Sometimes they sold things that were explicitly made to remind people that the things they bought were made with the labor of enslaved people—like tobacco boxes printed with anti-slavery iconography."

THE THINGS THEY MADE: PRETTY BUT WITH A POINT

The baby quilt with the poem in the middle was clearly made to spread the abolitionist message. What other things did abolitionist crafters craft? According to Mariah, "They range really widely. A lot of women would make a shawl or a lace-edged blanket. Pot holders, pincushions, needle cases. And maybe they would stitch a little something that would acknowledge the slavery cause, like 'May our needles prick the slaveholder's conscience.'" If you were a Boston housewife sewing things for the anti-slavery craft fair, it probably felt empowering to add on an anti-slavery message. Mariah says, "You could see something like a pincushion or a hankie as a thing where you could make a really bold and conscious political statement." Then when shoppers brought these pretty things home, they were spreading the anti-slavery message. Maybe others in the household—like the men who had more money and power—would get the message, too.

MONEY MEANS ACTION

Were the craft bazaars a success? "Financially they were incredible." Says Mariah, "They helped sustain anti-slavery activism." The Boston Fair was a yearly event before Christmas, other fairs followed suit. They ran from the 1830s into the 1850s. The fundraising "helped sustain publication of pamphlets, periodicals, and newspapers like *The Liberator*. And the money helped keep the anti-slavery societies afloat."

The fairs paid for people to go on speaking tours, activists like the Grimké Sisters. Mariah explains, "Sarah and Angelina Grimké grew up on a plantation with enslaved people and thought it was heinous and unacceptable. They talk about it like a conversion experience, the realization that it was immoral." The Grimkés were so horrified by what they saw growing up, how they saw Black people treated by white people, that they gave speeches at churches and town halls to convince others that slavery was wrong.

BUT IS IT LADYLIKE TO SPEAK UP?

Even though the Grimké sisters and the organizers of the craft fairs had money, they were still women. There were the Boston fairs, and Philadelphia had a female anti-slavery society and a fair, and there were many more groups. But these women's groups met with plenty of opposition. Women were expected to stay at home—and within their wife-and-motherly boundaries. I ask Mariah what these women were up against. What kinds of risks were they taking by joining the anti-slavery societies?

"There were huge risks to involvement," says Mariah. "In 1835, a mob attacked a female anti-slavery society meeting in Boston and almost killed one of the speakers." Women's anti-slavery societies might have stones thrown through their windows, and might face attacks as they left their meetings. Ladies who spoke out at meetings risked mockery and humiliation. They could lose their standing in communities. They might be attacked in newspapers. "The press would suggest that they had essentially failed to live up to their role as women (moral guardians of the home) by becoming involved in politics."

Mariah points out that "it's important to note, though, that this kind of risk would have been felt more acutely by Black women, who had far less social protection in these spaces than their white compatriots did."

While public activism could be tough for women, crafting allowed them to take action privately, quietly—and still have an impact. The anti-slavery societies encouraged everyday women to donate crafts, like a shawl or a stitched sampler. Every sale helped.

RACISM WITHIN ANTI-SLAVERY SOCIETIES

"Sincere anti-slavery activists could be racist," Mariah points out. Many activists believed that slavery was a sin or morally wrong, but they still did not see Black people as equals. "There was honest, real interracial cooperation in some of these groups. And very much not in others."

Mariah tells me that the first female anti-slavery society in the United States was formed by Black women. "In 1832, a group of 'females of color' (as they called themselves) in Salem, Massachusetts, formed the Female Anti-Slavery Society of Salem. They re-formed in 1834 as the Salem Female Anti-Slavery Society, an interracial organization." There were Black women in other anti-slavery societies as well, and they faced real discrimination.

Several anti-slavery societies were explicitly white-only. So—understandably—many Black women chose to start their own anti-slavery organizations. Mariah says, "There were two female anti-slavery groups in Rochester, New York—one Black and one white." The Boston Female Anti-Slavery Society was technically interracial, but they had segregated seating and were not run fairly, leaving the Black women frustrated.

ANTI-SLAVERY HELP (AND HINDRANCE) IN OTHER COUNTRIES

Mariah told me about a woman from Halifax, Canada, "who sent a blanket she made to a fair [in America] and said, 'I realize that you have more slaves in your country than I have stitches on this blanket and I thought of it with every stitch.'"

The British basically outlawed slavery in 1833, so abolitionist women in England started helping the cause over in America. They sewed needle bags and crafted other items for the anti-slavery craft fairs—some with messages on them, some without.

A group of American women went to the World Anti-Slavery Convention in London in 1840. They went to fight slavery, and in doing so, they faced sexism. Mariah explains, "They were not allowed to speak or be seated on the floor [of the convention space]. Even though these women were sent by the American abolitionists, they were not accepted. In a way, that has been seen as the start of the women's movement."

TWO PATHS TO ABOLITION

The American Anti-Slavery Society split in 1840 over the very question of women's involvement. One side left women out in order to get candidates elected to office. Women couldn't vote yet, and they definitely couldn't hold office.

The other side *did* include women. They were Garrisonian abolitionists—named for newspaperman and leader William Lloyd Garrison. The Garrisonian abolitionists sponsored people on speaking tours. They tried to help people who had escaped slavery and keep them safe. They published several abolitionist magazines, including one for children called *The Slave's Friend*. It taught kids to make crafts and showed images of Black and white kids in school together, playing together.

An anti-slavery magazine for children from the mid-1800s

ABOLITIONIST CRAFT FAIRS: ENDING AND EVOLVING

I wish I could say that the anti-slavery craft fairs ended because slavery ended, but that's not true. Mariah explains, "Honestly, they fell apart before the Civil War began. Partly due to personality conflicts between leaders, partly because by the 1850s it was less about selling crafts." Some local craft fairs still raised money to fight slavery. The Boston anti-slavery fair evolved into more of a fundraising gala event. Some of the anti-slavery women's groups focused on sewing directly for formerly enslaved people who needed clothes.

"Throughout the Civil War," says Mariah, "women continued to sew clothes and bandages for soldiers and to make things like tents, blankets, et cetera. Women also sewed beautiful quilts to send to soldiers, hoping that they would be reminded of home."

But many women discovered political activism from their anti-slavery work, and continued to fight for a better world. In fact, many organizers of female anti-slavery groups helped organize the first women's right's convention in Seneca Falls, New York, in 1848.

FROM THEN TO NOW

Pre–Civil War, American women generally knew some stitching skills, whether it was to mend things around the farmhouse or to fill leisure time. They were expected to learn to do some needlework. It was a key part of their femininity. The anti-slavery craft fairs meant women could take their stitching skills and use them in a new way—to raise money and consciousness.

Now learning to embroider or make lace is a choice, not an obligation. But there is still an interesting friction in using needlework for political causes. "It's helpful to know that people have been playing with this juxtaposition for hundreds of years," says Mariah. As a historian, she thinks about this a lot. How that tension is powerful. "Contemporary craftivists are taking part in a very long tradition of reframing the meanings of 'domestic' craft. They are working in different contexts, but those layered historical associations are still embedded in their stitches."

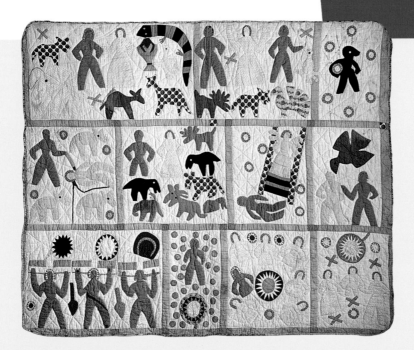

Harriet Powers, once enslaved, showed this Bible Quilt in 1886.

A BLACK AMERICAN QUILTER AND HER WORK

Between 1525 and 1866, an estimated 12.5 million people were forcibly taken from African countries to be sold into slavery in the New World. They were taken from their families, their cultures, their countries. It was difficult for enslaved people to carry on the art and language of countries they were forced to leave behind. But culture and creativity were not 100 percent destroyed in this horrific chapter of American history.

For example, a woman named Harriet Powers was born into slavery near Athens, Georgia, in 1837. She probably learned quiltmaking from her mother or other enslaved workers. Harriet was freed at the end of the Civil War. She married Armstead Powers while still young. They owned and ran a farm. Harriet probably made quilts her whole life but just two remain, including this gorgeous Bible Quilt. Harriet hand- and machine-stitched this quilt in 1885, then showed it at a cotton fair in 1886. It tells Christian stories such as (top row) Adam and Eve with the serpent in the Garden of Eden, (middle row) Cain killing Abel, Jacob's Ladder, and (bottom row) the Last Supper.

Harriet used applique technique, cutting out the shapes from one kind of fabric and stitching those shapes onto a base fabric. (Look at how the dots fabric shows up over and over again, as animals and also the sides of the ladder.) Historians have compared Harriet's bold appliqué style to that of the West African textiles from the Fon people of Abomey in a country that is now Benin, near Nigeria. (See the Abomey textile for comparison.)

Though Harriet's artistic style seems to connect to her ancestral culture, her images are from Bible stories important to her in her own day.

West African Abomey quilt, made with appliqué technique much like Harriet Powers' Bible quilt

A Southern white woman named Jennie Smith saw the Bible Quilt at the 1886 fair, sought out Harriet, and offered to buy it. But Harriet would not sell at any price. About four years later, after hitting on hard times—Harriet had at least nine children—Harriet reluctantly wrapped her quilt in a flour sack, put it in an oxcart, and sold it to Jennie Smith for five dollars. Jennie documented all the stories the quilt portrayed, and kept in touch with Harriet over the years.

Today Harriet Powers' Bible Quilt belongs to The National Museum of American History, as a stunning example of 1800s post–Civil War textile art. The quilt is so famous, there are kits for sale so quilters can make their own reproduction. Or just cut out figures from fabric to tell a story, tuck the edges of the shapes under, and stitch onto a quilt square. Harriet Powers would probably be proud.

Chapter Nine

AIDS Memorial Quilt

(1987–present)

To mourn and to celebrate those lost to AIDS, people joined the ultimate sewing circle. They made tribute panels for the AIDS Quilt. It's measured in acres, and still growing. Probably the biggest communal art project in history.

THE OLD-SCHOOL SUPERHERO OF CRAFTIVIST PROJECTS

In many ways, the AIDS Memorial Quilt inspired this book. When I tell people I'm writing about politics and handicrafts, I often get puzzled looks. Then I say, "Like the AIDS Quilt." Then they say, "Oh, right!" in recognition.

Anyone can make a panel to honor someone who died of AIDS. No training required, just compassion and 3 x 6 feet of fabric. Then the many panels together make a greater whole—for a cause. You almost cannot tell the story of the fight against AIDS without talking about the Quilt. It's part of history.

First display of the AIDS Memorial Quilt in Washington, DC, 1987

WHAT IS HIV/AIDS?

For younger readers, born after the peak of the AIDS crisis (a crisis that's not over), here are some basics. HIV stands for "human immunodeficiency virus." This virus is usually passed on through unprotected sex. HIV can be passed on in other ways, like through contact with infected body fluids from needle sharing, blood transfusions, mother-to-child in pregnancy, birth, or breastfeeding. HIV cannot be passed on through saliva, sweat, or tears. A person with HIV can remain symptom-free for a long time. But if left untreated, HIV can lead to AIDS. AIDS stands for "acquired immunodeficiency syndrome," which means the body loses some ability to fight infection. People with AIDS can get sick when opportunistic infections take over, like tuberculosis, tumors, and pneumonia. There is no cure or vaccine for AIDS (though there have been a few experimental cases of HIV being reversed—so there is hope). There are now medicines that help people with HIV live long, healthy lives. These life-extending drugs did not exist in the 1980s, when HIV and AIDS were first identified. It's been a long journey, and the AIDS Memorial Quilt played a part in raising awareness and money for research and treatments.

MY BRUSH WITH GREATNESS

I had the privilege of seeing a part of the AIDS Memorial Quilt up close at New York University, before it went on display. It was like meeting a rock star in their dressing room before a big show.

The Quilt is organized into 12' x 12' blocks made up of smaller 3' x 6' panels sewn together. I saw block #0154. The curator at NYU laid the section of panels out onto a big table and unfolded it like a flag. It has a panel for NYU and one for Bronx Community College, remembering students from those schools who died of AIDS. Plus panels for individuals who died of AIDS—Soren, Kenneth Davis, Larry Goode, Frank Sordi—people I'll never meet. But somebody who loved them sewed a bright sun, crisp clear letters, and a rainbow of hearts. What stayed with me were the hand-

Me documenting a section of the AIDS Memorial Quilt

written notes on the college panels. People signed them like a yearbook: "You were the greatest, you'll always be in my heart." Except yearbooks don't usually have messages like "Rest in peace, we'll love and miss you," or "Matt, I wish I had known before 'the end' so I could have said goodby [sic]," dated 2–15–90. These are young people writing to young people. Missing their friends.

The signatures on this AIDS Memorial Quilt panel remind me of a yearbook.

Panels made by college students in 1990 to honor friends lost to AIDS

BACKSTORY: SAN FRANCISCO IN THE 1970S

Back in the 1970s, the gay rights movement was gaining momentum, especially in San Francisco. Many LGBTQ people were drawn there. (Back then, there was no such acronym for lesbian, gay, bisexual, transgender, and queer—people mainly identified as "gay" or "queer.") They were seeking a more open and accepting community, away from the homophobia they faced in their hometowns. In 1977, Harvey Milk was voted in to the San Francisco Board of Supervisors, making him one of the first openly gay elected officials in the country. He was a charming leader who brought people together and fought for gay rights. His intern was a young gay activist named Cleve Jones.

On November 27, 1978, Harvey Milk was assassinated. He and San Francisco mayor George Moscone were shot down in City Hall by Dan White, a former supervisor who had voted against gay rights. It seemed like the whole city mourned. That night, thousands of people—gay and straight—filled the streets and held a candlelight vigil.

ORIGIN TALE: INSPIRATION STRIKES

Each year, on the anniversary of the assassination of Milk and Moscone, Cleve Jones helped organize a memorial candlelight vigil. Jones even used Harvey Milk's old bullhorn to address the crowds. For the 1985 vigil, Jones handed out squares of cardboard and markers and asked marchers to write out names of anyone they'd lost to this scary new disease called AIDS (or acquired immunodeficiency syndrome). By 1985, AIDS had killed over one thousand people in San Francisco. But numbers and statistics can feel cold and impersonal. Jones felt it would be more meaningful to see the names of the people who died, and to remember them as actual people. When the march ended that night, people taped their signs onto the outside wall of the San Francisco Federal Building. As Cleve Jones explains in the 2014 documentary *The Last One*, "I got to the edge of the crowd and I looked back over the crowd and all these people standing and looking at that patchwork of names and I thought to myself, 'It looks like some kind of strange quilt.' It was perfect."

America's first openly gay elected official, Harvey Milk, was assassinated in San Francisco in 1978. The idea for the AIDS Quilt began at a 1985 candlelight vigil to honor Milk's memory.

In that moment, Jones got the idea to create a quilt for those who had died of AIDS. Quilts tell the stories of a family, and this was a new family story that needed to be told. Jones wanted to take the squares from the wall and make them into something soft and also something powerful to show the world. He wanted to tell the story of the gay and queer family he'd become part of in San Francisco.

LET THE SEWING BEGIN

In June 1987, without much sewing experience, Cleve Jones made the first quilt panel to honor his best friend who had died of AIDS, Marvin Feldman. Then Jones teamed up with Mike Smith and Gert McMullin and others to officially start the AIDS Memorial Quilt. They called for people to honor loved ones lost to AIDS with a 3' x 6' fabric block bearing names and remembrances of all kinds—embroidered, appliquéd, glued, glittered, and written on that fabric block. No art or sewing experience necessary. Cleve Jones and his band of quilters set up a work space with tables and sewing machines on Market Street in San Francisco. People could drop off what they had made, or stay and work on their panel. It was a chance to be with other people who cared, other people mourning the losses brought on by AIDS.

Word of this project spread, and quilt panels poured in from all over the country. The quilt needed as many panels as they could get, because there was a gay and lesbian rights march scheduled for the fall of 1987 in Washington, DC. And these craftivists planned to be seen and heard there. The AIDS Memorial Quilt would be better than any protest sign.

FIGHTING HATE WITH FABRIC

Meantime, the AIDS epidemic was spreading, getting deadlier every year. And without medical information, studies, or funding, the crisis would get worse. Which it did. The US Department of Health under President Ronald Reagan was slow to respond to the crisis. By 1984, AIDS affected more than 7,500 people in the US, and over 3,500 had died. But President Reagan never even mentioned the word until September 1985. His administration was slow to take action or spend money. Politicians openly spoke of AIDS as a "gay plague" and not a mainstream problem. The AIDS Memorial Quilt could help combat this thinking. Cleve Jones said that the Quilt "was never intended to be a passive memorial. It was created to be a weapon in our war against not only a disease but the cruelty and bigotry that the disease exposed."

A POWERFUL DEBUT

Fired up, the first wave of quilters made, collected, and sewed together almost two thousand panels in just over four months. The AIDS Memorial Quilt was first displayed on the National Mall in Washington, DC, to coincide with the National March on Washington for Gay and Lesbian Rights. On October 11, 1987, at dawn, forty-eight volunteers unfolded the AIDS Quilt, which covered more ground than a football field. Celebrities, politicians, lovers, friends, and family members read the names of the dead out loud. Half a million people came to see the Quilt that first weekend.

The flood of emotions and support from the public inspired organizers to take the Quilt on a twenty-city tour throughout the spring and summer of 1988. Wherever they brought the Quilt, people added panels, tripling the Quilt's size by the end of the tour. This act of craftivism raised almost $500,000 for AIDS research and related causes. And this was just the first year.

Washington, DC, 1996, the last time the entire AIDS Memorial Quilt was on display in one place

Julie Rhoad was there in the early days of the Quilt, then worked to preserve its legacy.

THE GROWING WORK OF POLITICAL ART

By October 1988, there were over eight thousand panels. In 1989, the AIDS Memorial Quilt was nominated for a Nobel Peace Prize. The last time the entire AIDS Memorial Quilt was displayed all together was in 1996, when it covered the entire Washington, DC, National Mall. Cleve Jones walked among the quilt panels with President Bill Clinton and First Lady Hillary Clinton. Said Jones of that moment, "I remember the feeling that there actually was hope."

Since then, the Quilt became too big to display in one place. Now smaller sections travel all over the country, displayed in churches, offices, malls, museums, universities—like the panels I saw at NYU. Broken up into smaller sections, the Quilt can reach more people, spread its message further. The AIDS Memorial Quilt is the largest community art project in the world, and it's still growing.

THE KEEPER OF THE QUILT

I spoke with Julie Rhoad, the President and CEO of the NAMES Project Foundation/AIDS Memorial Quilt from 2001 to 2020. She had the huge job of overseeing this activist art piece, tracking it, preserving it, and presenting it to the world. Julie, who has been involved with the Quilt since the very early days, helped me understand the history and meaning of this important work of craftivism.

BIG FOR A REASON

As a quilter myself, I had to ask why the panels of the AIDS Memorial Quilt are so big. Quilts are usually made up of smaller scraps and squares. Was it so people could see the work from a distance? "That was very intentional," Julie explains. "Three feet by six feet approximates a human grave. You have to think about what society was saying at that time. Calling out the disease and saying, 'It was those

Memorial panels are sewn together in groups of eight.

wild gay people.' Talking about statistics and numbers, not souls and human beings." Each panel is a metaphorical grave, because so many people did not get buried or honored in the way they deserved. Many who died of AIDS were disconnected from or rejected by their families.

"Cleve's idea was to create a quilt because quilts keep you warm. They repurpose old clothes and give you information about your family. I worked in the theater community, where gay people were accepted. It's your adult family. You spend six days a week together. They are your people you go out to dinner with. With the advent of the AIDS epidemic, we became a care team. A lot of people who were gay moved from small-town America to large cities. Many times I had to call a mother or a father and let them know that their child was sick or dead at the same time they were learning they were gay. Their families would scoop up the bodies and we had no place to grieve."

A BEAUTIFUL HOMEMADE CEMETERY

Cemeteries are places where the public comes to grieve, and to think about the dead. But what if the public is not grieving? What if the public is ignorant—willfully or not—about the tragedy that is all around them? What if ordinary citizens are not thinking about the dead? Then you bring the cemetery to them.

Julie tells me, "When Cleve's group of people got together to do this, they knew the march was going to happen. The second march for gay and lesbian equality. That October, they made sure they could lay out the dead so people could bear witness." In June 1987, they hung the first block on the mayor's balcony in San Francisco. It made national news. "I remember thinking about the number of people I needed to make quilt panels for the march. I did make panels and I'm not a sewer. But hand-in-hand we go."

ANGER IS GOOD MOTIVATION

Julie Rhoad, Cleve Jones, and a growing band of quilters got very busy. It happened so fast. From June to October 1987, almost two thousand names and panels were added to the Quilt. That seems almost impossible, but Julie remembers that time. "It started with eight people making panels to raise consciousness. We talk about coalition building and building alliances and political power. In 1987, there was no [government] voice for the gay community. People in Congress said that AIDS was God's smite on gay people and they all deserve to die."

Julie is not exaggerating. For example, in 1987, North Carolina Senator Jesse Helms fought to limit the way the government could fund AIDS education and treatment saying, "We've got to call a spade a spade and a perverted human being a perverted human being."

The Quilt was a response to Helms and others. "Having a place for people to express their sorrow and their anger and say, 'We have got to do more and face this tragedy.' That motivated us." Says Julie, "Having the moms and dads and aunts come to DC and speak for the gay community. The Quilt helped make this possible."

FOUNDED ON TRADITION

"Everything you can think about a quilt applies here," says Julie. "It's made with many hands together gathered about a table, and when you gather at a quilting bee, you talk." Quilting together is therapeutic, especially when it opens the door to conversations that were hard to have anywhere else. "HIV and AIDS are very painful, difficult, isolating topics," says Julie. "One of the softest ways into the discussion of sexuality, pain, and suffering is a quilt. The quilt is a soft way in. It does what art does: It reminds us of our humanity. You can connect to the quilt something familiar—your love of cats or dogs, your zip code. There's something in a panel you can connect with. If you see that you are connected, you might see the big picture that says we are all connected. And then maybe you can get inspired to act. Then you can see that maybe we are responsible for each other."

YET BLOWING UP TRADITION

Before the 1980s, quilting was mostly considered the realm of grandmothers and homebodies. It was not the chosen art form for political rebels. But Julie points out, "the AIDS Quilt revolutionized quilting and the notion of quilting. Up until then, quilts had particular patterns and particular kinds of stitching and batting, but the AIDS Quilt makes a three-by-six-foot story of a loved one." And Julie explains how normal quilting rules do not apply to the AIDS Quilt. "It's a remarkable thing. Some people paint their panels. Some people stitch photographs on. Lots of cats, lots of bells. Someone attached a bowling ball. Someone attached an air-conditioning vent. Hospital humor. You have to find a way to laugh."

BEYOND AMERICAN

The HIV/AIDS epidemic is not just an American problem—it is a global one. Though the numbers have been going down, there were still over 37 million people living with HIV worldwide in 2020. I wondered if this very American-style act of craftivism has spread to other countries. Julie tells me, "This quilt is predominantly domestic, but we have panels from over one hundred different countries. Other chapters have formed globally. So Canada has an AIDS Quilt, England and Amsterdam have Quilts. South Africa has one, but it's a little different. Young kids were messaging from township to township, like writing 'Use a condom' on their panels." They were using the Quilt as a billboard, as well as a memorial. Sometimes ideas change and evolve as they travel.

MAKING QUILT PANELS TODAY

The AIDS Memorial Quilt website (aidsmemorial.org) has instructions on how to make a memorial panel. Julie tells me, "We get on average about a panel a day. But the majority come in when someone has seen a display, when someone is ready to let go of a panel they held on to for years. Or someone whose favorite uncle died. Or someone younger is exploring the family history and they want to make a panel for someone who died. The next generation is telling the stories. We get about three hundred a year. In a peak year, up to eight hundred." As of September 2021, there were just over 50,000 panels, 6,007 blocks, and 105,000 names.

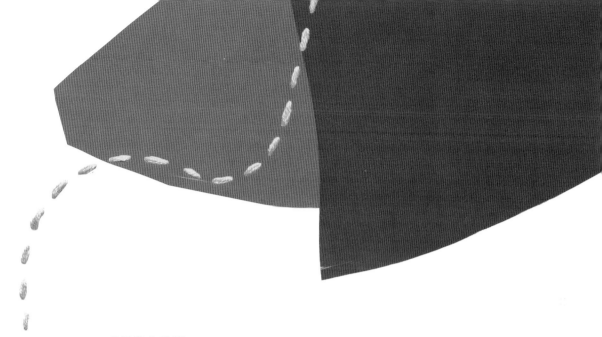

LEGACY

What makes the AIDS Memorial Quilt so amazing to me is this: It's both a historical document and a still-growing work of craftivism. Julie agrees. "It's a remarkable work of collective art. It's a memorial that illustrates democracy like no other. It's 'by the people for the people' they love. Not one artist, not a committee. When you think about monuments, they are about the heroes, not the everyday people. But this is an interesting twist. The people remembered in the panels are the heroes to us."

Julie adds, "The quilt itself is both intimate and epic. These really potent stories of life and love are compelling on their own. If you start to group them together in a twelve-by-twelve-foot section, it starts to become epic. It tells a truth. We have to make sure these stories are told from generation to generation because we cannot let this happen again."

Chapter Ten

Social Justice Sewing Academy

(2017–present)

Quilting the truth: Young people who have a lot to say about their country learn to say it with fabric.

POWER OF QUILTING

Quilters don't just decorate, they transform old into new. Jeans get cut up to form letters. Pieces of an old green shirt become leaves of a flower. Then there's the quilting bee. It makes sense to sit at a big table and work on your quilt square—or "block" in quilting lingo. It's satisfying, it's social. Quilts have been made this way for centuries. At Social Justice Sewing Academy (SJSA), young people learn this very old textile tradition and use it to express their very current ideas. The quilters of SJSA are ready to see society change.

SOCIAL JUSTICE SEWING ACADEMY 101

Sara Trail founded the Social Justice Sewing Academy in 2017. Sara and her team lead workshops all around the country, but mostly in the Bay Area of California.

They teach quilt-making in schools, prisons, and community centers, anywhere they can connect with students who need to be heard. In the workshops, young people discuss politics and community issues. They talk about problems that affect their lives and what they'd like to see change.

Then the workshoppers take their ideas and express them through textile art. They design and cut out the words and shapes to make quilt blocks, like signs in a march. They have messages about gender inequality, racism, gun violence, gentrification, police brutality, and more. The designs are secured into place by volunteers all over the country who embroider the blocks and then send them back to the Academy, where more volunteers sew the squares together to form the full quilt. In the end, many hands, many people who don't know each other, work on the quilt because they all care about the kids who started it.

SJSA students, often new to sewing, express themselves with fabric.

An SJSA block I worked on. A scary image for a scary issue.

HOW I DISCOVERED SJSA

I heard about SJSA from a craft-loving teacher at my kids' NYC public school. The SJSA quilt blocks posted online had bright slogans and illustrations, and spoke of problems like colorism and mass incarceration. I saw refreshing visual takes on issues like gender, harassment, and voting rights.

I have since become a volunteer for SJSA, stitching and embellishing quilt blocks that someone else designed. Here's one I helped with, above. To be honest, when I opened the envelope from SJSA, the image scared me. It looked like a spider or a Nazi swastika over a target.

But as I worked with the block and really sat with it, I realized that it's *supposed* to be jarring. The artist was making the point that guns are scary and dangerous. Message received. SJSA encourages volunteers to add our creative voices to the artwork, so I embroidered the circle of red drops (blood) because I'm scared of guns, too. I was collaborating with someone I never met. I still don't know who started this piece—their name, age, gender, or anything else about them—but I'm proud of our work together.

SARA TRAIL, FOUNDER OF SOCIAL JUSTICE SEWING ACADEMY

The founder and leader of SJSA is Sara Trail. She invented this collaborative quilt-making process. Sara is an impressive combination of artist and thinker, organizer and doer. I was thrilled to ask her about her art-activism.

Sara has been sewing since the age of four. She published a sewing book at thirteen, and created her own fabric collection at age fifteen. Sara says, "I was leading classes, teaching other kids to sew. But around age fifteen, sixteen, I started noticing the capitalism and privilege. The kids I taught had to have seventy-five dollars and a sewing machine. Only affluent white kids could come. I wanted to teach all kinds of kids. Kids who didn't have those things."

Sara Trail, Founder of Social Justice Sewing Academy

HEADLINES INSPIRE ART

Sara has noticed class inequality since way back. But there was a key moment when Sara connected her art with the fight for social change. She explains, "It was when Trayvon Martin got killed, it was my freshman year in college. I was working on a Double Wedding Ring quilt." In 2012, Trayvon Martin, a seventeen-year-old Black high school student, was visiting his dad at a gated community in Florida when he was shot and killed by a man named George Zimmerman, who was on neighborhood watch. Trayvon was unarmed, and Zimmerman walked free. The story exploded in the news and led to protests, petitions, and student walkouts. Sara remembers, "I had this moment of

'What am I spending my time doing? Why am I making a wedding ring quilt?' I started working on the Trayvon quilt. I stopped buying patterns, and following instructions. I wanted to accomplish this on my own." Sara dumped her old quilt templates—the Double Wedding Ring is a traditional American quilt pattern, hundreds of years old—and didn't look back.

"Trayvon was the first time I made the quilt without a quilt pattern. No one was going to make that pattern. In 2012, the quilt business was not about political quilts. I mean, people made quilts for homeless people and baby blankets—for public service. But this quilt was about expressing my feelings, my anger." Sara merged her passion for quilts with her passion for justice. Sara's first political quilt forces us to look Trayvon right in the eye and reckon with the safety we, as a country, were unable to provide for him. It's not meant to be cozy. It's a tribute to someone who's gone. It's a reminder of what needs to change.

Sara's first political quilt, a portrait of Trayvon Martin, an unarmed teen killed in 2012

SEWING AND KNOWING

Sara wanted to share her passion for community issues and self-expression. So she got a grant from UC Berkeley and reached out to high school students in the area. "I knew how to teach sewing construction. That was really simple for me. I had been teaching sewing for a long time. But I wanted to teach about ideas, too. It was as much about education as it was about sewing. We read James Baldwin, Toni Morrison. I took what I was learning in my classes in Berkeley, I annotated it and turned it around and I gave it to the high school kids. They engaged with it. These are texts we still use in our workshops. A lot of schools are really Eurocentric. So we try to read Indigenous authors, queer authors, Black authors."

Sara's passion for teaching led her to pursue a graduate degree in education from Harvard. Then she came back to California and founded the Social Justice Sewing Academy, where she inspires new thinkers and craftivists to this day.

HOW THE WORKSHOPS WORK

There's not a brick-and-mortar building for the Social Justice Sewing Academy. Sara brings the workshops to the people—at schools, churches, and community centers. Most of her students have never quilted. I ask her what it's like to work with new quilters, and to teach them this kind of art-activism. Sara says, "Fabric and textile is a great place to begin. Everyone's familiar with it. Clothes are something you put on every day. Fabric is something you've touched all your life. Not everyone has worked with clay, but everyone has touched fabric."

Every student makes a fifteen-inch block with their message and illustration, something that expresses what they feel. The students cut out the words and images, and then glue them in place, like a collage or protest poster made with fabric. Quilting is traditionally collaborative, like an old-fashioned quilting bee. Some of that quilting bee tradition carries through to the SJSA sessions. "At the workshops, it's both individual and collaborative," Sara explains. "You can get help from other people. One person might be good at making hair, another person is good at cutting letters. Asking your neighbor for help is part of it. You say, 'Thanks for cutting it out,' but you have agency. You decide how you want to use it, or where it goes. The core aspect of your design is up to you. It isn't finalized until you say it's final. The block is about what matters to you, what you want to see change."

YOUNG TEACHING OLD

After student quilters lay out their textile blocks, the Social Justice Sewing Academy mails the blocks to volunteers like me. Volunteers secure the design with embroidery, and another level of collaboration begins. "We have embroidery volunteers from all over. That's a lot of work by hand and that's time spent, so we appreciate it."

The students in the workshops are generally young, a lot of kids of color, in a lot of challenging situations. I'm sure that many of the volunteers are older white ladies—like me—who might not have a personal connection to the messages on the quilt blocks. So I ask Sara how the volunteers respond to the messages in the quilt squares. "The Bay Area is pretty woke," she says, "but the embroidery volunteers are learning what the kids are thinking about. There are blocks about colorism and some people don't know what that is." Sara explains that colorism within Black communities "is prejudice that the closer you are to white the better you are. That's colorism: the lighter you are the better." Even toy stores are sending out the message that pale skin is the "right" color to be. "Growing up, I never had a Barbie that looks like me." Black dolls are harder to find, and if you do their skin is usually light brown, not dark.

Sara says, "One of our volunteers got a block that said 'Don't touch my hair,' and the woman said, 'I don't get it.' So I said, 'Look into it. But it's about consent.' So the lady did, and she told me later, 'I was crying. I have done that so many times. You have to ask, and I've done it so many times.'" Sara goes on to explain, "My friend

A full quilt made up of many SJSA quilt blocks

with dreads says that women, especially older women, touch her hair because they like it. It's hard to tell them not to, but that's consent." Because of a quilt block, a volunteer asked some questions and learned a thing or two in the process. That is activism—and actual change—through craft. The quilters are spreading a message even before the quilt is done. Sara says, "Volunteers are embroidering on the bus, then other people ask about it. We send a quilt block to Betty in Arkansas and then her friends want to do one, too."

FINISHING THE SOCIAL JUSTICE QUILTS

The volunteers like me mail the embellished quilt blocks back to SJSA, where more volunteers add borders and assemble the squares to form the quilt front. Then they sandwich the layers, bind the edges, and quilt it all together. (The verb "quilting" is the technical term for stitching all the layers together.) "Then," Sara explains, "we put a label on it. We send it back to the kids that made it. Every kid writes an artist statement. We are giving them agency."

A NEW GENERATION OF QUILTERS

"I think quilting has the monolithic identity of being a grandma hobby," says Sara. "You can learn from your grandma. As a hobby, you learn from someone older. But here we are flipping the narrative. The kids are in the driver's seat and we give them creative license. In our workshops, at the end of the day, the adults know the stitches, but we are giving kids an opportunity to express themselves with textile."

Ahmaud Arbery, killed in 2020 while jogging, unarmed. Quilted block by Martha Wolfe for the SJSA Remembrance Project.

I ask Sara if student quilts with statements about gun violence or poverty or rape—topics that are not soft and cuddly like grandma quilts—ever shock people. She says, "Most of the reactions are positive. Most people like it. But there are people who are like, 'Why are you teaching so much hate?' and 'You need to come up with solutions.' 'The quilts are disturbing.' But if you are a mom, you have a kid going to public school doing a lockdown drill, you know these are the issues of today. Ignorance is blind. This is what inner-city kids are thinking. Let's hear it. There's something healthy in expressing anger. It's more than anger. It's a critique and a vision of hope."

IT DIDN'T END WITH TRAYVON

Sara sewed a quilt to honor Trayvon Martin in 2012. In the years since, more young unarmed Black men have been killed at an alarming rate. In 2020, the public murder of an unarmed man named George Floyd by Minneapolis police sparked Black Lives Matter (BLM) protests nationwide. That summer, in the spirit of and support of the BLM movement, the Social Justice Sewing Academy launched a new quilting project to "remember the lives lost due to social injustices." It's called the SJSA Remembrance Project. Much like the AIDS Memorial Quilt, SJSA invites craftivists to make a 22" x 26" fabric block that names and honors someone who was murdered in a politically or racially motivated manner. That is, murdered by authorities (police, security guards), community (gang violence, family violence), race (hate crimes), or gender and sexuality (LGBTQ, missing indigenous women, etc). These blocks are then assembled into quilts and banners that community organizations can display. The banners can also travel to marches, "as they work to bring attention to the injustices faced by people and communities nationwide."

A NAME, A START

I ask Sara if she calls what she teaches "craftivism," "activism," or something else? She tells me she calls her students and volunteers "artivists." Sara explains, "This is art plus activism. It's about becoming an agent of social change."

What advice does Sara have for an artivist who's just getting started, someone who wants to try quilting for a cause? "Go to a fabric store and start with the scrap bin. Go to a thrift store and buy fabric and upcycle. Or use what you have. Cut clothes apart. Start creating. It's just like making a collage with paper, except it's fabric. Cut letters. Get needle and thread and start making something. Go on YouTube to try what you see people doing there. You don't have to color in the lines. There's no pattern. No experience necessary. Just create."

Beyond
Basic Crafts

Beyond Basic Crafts

Craftivism comes in many forms beyond needle and thread, hammer and nail. There are so many ways to make things, so many materials to use. Some you probably never thought of as forms of protest. The word "craftivism" is evolving, even within the art-activist community. To me, craftivism: 1) is doable with little or no training, 2) doesn't require fancy equipment, 3) is at least partly handmade, so there's some of your time and effort invested in each piece, and 4) has a goal in mind—even if it's just to start difficult or important conversations. Accessible. Doable. By the people, for the people. There's a project for everyone's skill set.

Sometimes you have to look a little harder to find the mode of expression that brings you joy. Meet artist-agitators who send out political messages by baking (yum!), taking photos (isn't there a camera in your pocket right now?), tagging the streets, and even gluing collages—all for a better world.

Chapter Eleven

Baking: The Sweet Feminist

(2018–present)

Becca Rea-Holloway is stirring up the revolution from her kitchen, baking protest cakes that speak truth to power.

It's a form of art-protest.

CRAFTIVISM WITH SUGAR ON TOP? YES, PLEASE

The closest I get to baking is putting a Pop-Tart in the toaster, and I still mess up the setting. I don't watch cooking shows or follow anything foodie on social media. Instead, I follow feeds about rag rug braiding and Japanese mending techniques. I follow politicians and political artists a-plenty. But nothing about food. My search for craftivists did not include bakers and cooks. Then, a friend who bakes steered me toward Becca Rea-Holloway, aka The Sweet Feminist. I found Becca's work online and became an instant admirer. Not because of her recipes (she has lots), but for her special mode of visual political protest: cakes. Also pies, cookies, and the occasional savory dish. Becca's main weapon is icing, and she wields it fearlessly.

WHAT THE SWEET FEMINIST DOES

Becca posts photos of gorgeous cakes and other treats with provocative words on them. She asks the hard questions, but in bright colors on something delicious. The contrast between the hard news and the sweet treats is striking and interesting. An attention grabber, and that's the point.

Becca's protest cakes have messages about the news ("STOP CALLING THE POLICE"), things not in the news enough ("PRISON IS A PUBLIC HEALTH EMERGENCY," "STATEHOOD FOR DC"), pop culture ("NO CAKE FOR DRAKE" due to Drake's collaboration with Chris Brown), helpful reminders ("DON'T FORGET TO STEP OUTSIDE YOUR OWN EXPERIENCE") and sometimes just plain rage ("FUCK YOU PAY ME"). Becca's messages open conversations that are thought-provoking and informative. Her followers can learn about climate and gender and consent and even the Constitution from comments on her posts. Who knew frosting could bring about change?

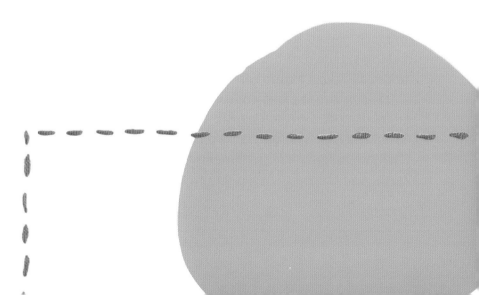

Becca Rae-Holloway, The Sweet Feminist

BECOMING THE SWEET FEMINIST

I like to know every superhero's origin story. Was Becca bitten by a sugar cube? Becca has never taken a baking class. She first learned from watching her grandmother in the kitchen, then continued to teach herself. I ask Becca what her grandmother thinks of her baking-activism. "I have never really asked. She's a strong power and really fun. I assume she would love it."

Even before she was an icing activist, Becca worked in sales and marketing for a Washington, DC, bakery. Baking was what she loved and she did it on her own time, too. But how did she become The Sweet Feminist? "I wanted to express my views and frustrations. And I thought, 'What do I already do anyway? I bake cakes.' I wanted to do a new thing that could reach a different group of people: people interested in baking, and feminists. Capture both in one thing. I got this idea to start writing on cakes. It's a short format. You are limited by a medium that only fits a few words. People are used to seeing words on cake."

Yes, people are used to seeing "HAPPY ANNIVERSARY" or "CONGRATULATIONS, GRADUATE!" Most people associate cakes with joy and celebration. Then I see a Sweet Feminist cake that says "ABOLISH ICE" and it messes with my head. In a good way. "Exactly," says Becca. "I write messages that push people. Then you can expand in the [social media] caption. Some things will challenge people more. And some messages are more palatable—so you are meeting people where they are at. Maybe they don't have much experience with feminism but are interested. When I post, it opens a conversation. I learn from people's comments and answers, too. Sometimes I'm wrong, and that's okay. I personally have learned a lot."

FINDING HER AUDIENCE, WRITING A HIT

In the age of social media, you can sit in your room alone, hit that "post" button, and send a message out into the world. Like launching a rocket into space. Will it be a disaster? Is anyone even watching? Becca knows all about this. She has received a range of reactions to her Sweet Feminist posts. "One of the values of this project is that it's very shareable. You can share it and you can say, 'We both understand this experience.' It gives people a visual to express things they feel. Or it helps them experience things they might not on their own. It's great to see how many people my cakes resonate with. Way more than I anticipated."

One cake she posted that got a huge positive reaction says "IMMIGRANTS MAKE AMERICA GREAT." That's one of her biggest hits, so far. "People shared that one a lot," says Becca. "It really resonated with a lot of people." Which immigrants did people take it to mean? Themselves? Their parents? The people in their city? The general idea? "All of that," says Becca, smiling.

One of the Sweet Feminist cakes that went viral

AND ALSO PISSING PEOPLE OFF . . . WITH CAKE

"I got pushback on my 'CANCEL MEN 2019' cake," says Becca. Not just any pushback—the post was flagged as hate speech. But The Sweet Feminist stands by her words. "I think hyperbolic, bigger-than-life language is fine. I'm prompting a dialogue. I'm also expressing something I feel in certain moments." She's drawing fire on purpose to get an important conversation going. She wants us to look at the ugly truth. It doesn't mean she's living this feeling 24/7. "Of course you can love men in your life, but can still work to deconstruct the power dynamic where men have more say than women. We still live with that."

HATERS HATING

Becca clearly welcomes opposing opinions. She's all about having a conversation. But she also knows what's useful and what's pointless. Becca tells me, "I was getting middle school and high school guys saying stuff like 'Make me a sandwich.' I think it's testing boundaries and group bonding. It made me really angry and it made me sad to see that. I would just delete them. I think for them it's about asserting power over women and girls. They liked to see the reaction, to be inflammatory. I didn't respond, but then my followers would argue." After a while, Becca limited her online comments to people who followed her, and hasn't looked back.

But she still listens to opposition, and is open to changing her mind. "Being accountable publicly is hard," says Becca. "But I'm trying to set an example. I try not to change a post. If I realize I'm wrong or adjust my view, I try to add it as a comment so you can see the progression of ideas."

EMBRACING THE F-WORD

Even before I looked at a single one of Becca's cakes, the Sweet Feminist name got my attention. It surprised me, because a lot of younger women I know retreat from the word "feminist." Maybe because "feminism" conjures up the image of angry bra-burning hippies with armpit hair. Maybe because feminism is not considered feminINE. Or maybe it's because feminism has historically been led by upper-middle-class white women. And people who were poor, trans, queer, and women of color were not fully taken into account in the movement. To me, feminism means women, or anyone who identifies as something other than male, deserve the same rights and privileges as men. And a feminist is anyone who agrees. Becca says, "I think it's important for feminism to be an all-encompassing term, not just focused on white, young, cis ["cis" means identifying as the gender you were assigned at birth], able-bodied women. I have had to clarify that. I like expanding the idea of who feminism is for—it's for everybody."

WOMEN IN THE KITCHEN

The Sweet Feminist once posted, "Women have always used creative arts like crafting and baking as sites of resistance, and I see my cakes as a continuation of that rich tradition." Becca's activism seems modern to me, but I like the way she connects it to the past. I ask her about that quote and she explains, "Before there was social media, the domestic arts provided a place to come talk, to feel less isolated. Crafting and baking were arts that women were allowed to be experts on. Now I'm pushing the boundaries of what those arts can do."

Becca's cookies are as wise as her cakes.

STIR UP YOUR OWN BATTER

Even though The Sweet Feminist takes on hot-button issues, she still keeps it fun. Becca started this whole thing because she loves baking cakes. She now lives in Austin, Texas, and is working on a cookbook—all desserts of course—about baking your feelings. She wants to spread the gospel of self-expression through sweets. "Your message can be serious but your canvas doesn't have to be serious. All you need is a cake, frosting, and ideas." Becca enjoys other people's frosted statements. "I'll get messages from college groups and local Planned Parenthoods. They'll show me a picture of what they made. I love to see other people doing it. Not everybody can draw or sew, but cake decorating is doable. The more people, the better."

Sometimes it's hard to know where to begin. Maybe you want to make a message cake, but you're not sure what to say. For better or worse, there's no shortage of issues and events that deserve commentary. Becca remembers, "When I started, I started with a literal notebook of ideas. Things that happened to me that upset me, or things that happened to me that were great. You can make a cake from a box or frosting from a box. You can buy a cake. The cake itself is not as important. It's what you say on it."

I ask Becca what she's thinking up for future cakes, future messages. "I'm along for the ride. I'm taking things as they come. I don't have huge lofty goals. But . . . I would love a woman president. I would love to make a cake for a woman president."

Chapter Twelve

Photography: Las Fotos Project

(2010–present)

An after-school program in Los Angeles gives cameras to young women of color so they can show the world what they see. Because what they see matters.

Teen LFP student Maya took this photo of her brother and his girlfriend as they make an offering to the Virgin Mary on their way home from school. East LA, 2017.

Dorothea Lange's 1936 photo of a migrant worker

PHOTOGRAPHY BACKSTORY: CAPTURING THE REAL WORLD

No, it's not handicraft like sewing or carving, but photography is still a kind of making. And nearly anyone can try it. The art form is almost 200 years old.

Photography was invented in the 1830s, but the equipment was expensive and bulky. Exposure times were long. Starting around the 1880s, cameras got smaller and cheaper. Regular folks could take them out and about. Ever since then, people have been documenting the beautiful to help preserve it, and documenting the ugly so we don't forget it. This is photojournalism, but it's also art-activism, if you think about it.

During the Great Depression in the 1930s, the US government under President Franklin D. Roosevelt hired photographers to document poverty, especially rural poverty. FDR needed public support for his relief spending.

One of these photographers was a New Jersey woman named Dorothea Lange. In 1936, Lange took this portrait of a thirty-two-year-old mother, a migrant pea picker stranded in a camp in Northern California. When the photo was published, there was an emergency shipment of food sent to her encampment. Art brought change.

WHAT IS LAS FOTOS PROJECT?

Las Fotos Project (LFP) is a nonprofit community-based organization that offers free classes and workshops to female, female-identifying, and gender-fluid students of color, ages thirteen through eighteen, in Los Angeles. Their students get access to professional cameras and gear, and they work with artist mentors who help them develop their skills. Through photography, students explore their community and their own identity. They also learn an art form that can turn into a job someday.

Alyssa Garcia is a photographer and mentor to teen girls of color who take classes at Las Fotos Project in LA.

ALYSSA GARCIA EXPLAINS HOW LFP BEGAN

Alyssa Garcia began as a volunteer at Las Fotos Project. She tells me, "I started mentoring. I used to teach art and photography." Now Alyssa is the Director of Education and Programs at Las Fotos Project. She's still very involved with students and classes.

I ask Alyssa how LFP came to be. "We just celebrated our ten-year anniversary," she says proudly. "Our founder is a photographer named Eric V. Ibarra." Ibarra wanted to start an after-school program that focused on photography, so he reached out to a couple of Los Angeles schools that agreed to try it. "Then on the first day, [Ibarra] showed up and there were only girls there. And he thought, 'Okay, I have a bunch of nieces. I can do this.'" But later on, "when it was time for the girls to review their images, there were men around [like school staff, other students], and it definitely changed their vibe." So Ibarra decided to go full-fledged. "Only female-identified students of color." Alyssa says, "Also gender nonbinary and gender nonconforming." And that has been their student body ever since.

SHINING A LIGHT ON WHAT'S IMPORTANT IN THE COMMUNITY

As a photographer herself, Alyssa knows the power of choosing an image and sending it out into the world. Las Fotos Project actively encourages students to use photography to help their communities. Through photography, Alyssa says, "They can advocate on an issue that deserves to have light shown on it—like gentrification, food insecurity, green spaces, small business owners." A student can photograph a park that has too much garbage and needs a cleanup. They can show a local tailor or food cart that needs more business. Photographers are reporters and documentarians as well as artists—a camera is empowering. As Alyssa points out, "Capturing your community is advocating for yourself. That is one and the same."

LFP student Jacqi's 2017 photo of her local ice cream man. An important member of the community. Especially if you are a kid.

LOCAL BUSINESSES, LOCAL PEOPLE

Las Fotos Project student Jacqi took this photo of a man at the wheel of his truck in 2017. "We ask our photographers to highlight their day-to-day life," explains Alyssa. "That's their neighborhood ice cream man. It has that sense of coming of age. When you have enough money to get what you want. And you can maybe even buy some for your kid sister." When you are young, the ice cream man is very important. He treats you like a client and customer. This photo is clearly from the POV of a person buying the goods.

THE IMPORTANCE OF BEING SEEN

If you can't see something, you can't change it or fix it or celebrate it. Some of the students have parents and grandparents who are immigrants and are reluctant to appear in photographs. Maybe they are shy and used to being marginalized—which literally means off to the side, like in the margins of a page. But the teachers and mentors help LFP teens to document their elders and themselves. Everyone deserves to take up space and be seen.

EXPANDING THE IDEA OF SELF-PORTRAIT

A self-portrait doesn't have to include your face. Think about your bedroom. Doesn't it tell a lot about you? How neat or messy you are, what sports or music you're into, what colors you like, maybe how big or small your family is? Las Fotos Project encourages photographers to show who they are through objects around them and through the setting they live in.

A longer shutter speed makes this LA street corner blurry and dreamy.

MAKING THE ORDINARY EXTRAORDINARY

I am captivated by this photo of a stop sign. Alyssa tells me, "This is a study on shutter speed. You can modify the shutter speed and can adjust the angle to get different effects." Shutter speed is how long the film or digital sensor in the camera is exposed to light—sort of like blinking your eyes fast versus blinking slow. This photo was taken with the shutter open longer, making the image brighter and blurrier. And with that one choice, the corner looks dreamy and magical.

DIGITAL VS FILM

With smartphones in so many pockets, most people are somewhat familiar with digital photography. At Las Fotos Project, they use both digital and film cameras. Alyssa explains the importance of working with film, as a way to learn and think differently. "I started with film and I only shoot film. When you only have twenty-four to thirty-six exposures, you have to be more intentional. You have to make sure the settings are correct before you hit the button." With film photography, you don't see the results until later, when you develop your film. And when you see your prints, "it's like Christmas," says Alyssa.

An LFP student named Metzi took this in 2018. LA is a driving town and this steering wheel is part of a lowrider car in a Boyle Heights, LA, car club.

LAS FOTOS PROJECT ARTWORK: OUT IN THE WORLD

Las Fotos Project works with a media company that posts LFP photos on billboards and bus stops in the LA area. "We have our students' work in bus shelters in their community. It's different than having an art show up in a gallery where they have their class." It's the pride of being able to see their photos nearby, out in the world. Plus LFP is bringing art to people who might not see art. And Las Fotos Project has collaborations with the Getty Museum and the *LA Times*, which have featured LFP photography.

Las Fotos Project also has gallery shows at the end of each semester. Alyssa loves it when people step into the gallery space and say, "I wish that this had been around when I was younger."

GOOD FIRST ASSIGNMENT: TAKE A PHOTO WALK

I ask Alyssa about a good first project for a new photographer-activist. Something to try with a digital camera or even a disposable film camera. Alyssa describes a regular assignment at Las Fotos Project: "We do a lot of photo walks. We have our students take a walk around the neighborhood and capture the things that speak to them. One person showed trash. They photograph what they are drawn to in terms of advocacy." Another beginner challenge: "We ask students to take portraits of themselves without being in it."

Do you have a smartphone sitting near you as you read this? Then you have a camera. What are you waiting for? Try a photo walk or a non-selfie self-portrait.

Chapter Thirteen
Street Art: SacSix
(2015–present)

Graffiti is one of the oldest forms of self-expression. People posting their work in public to amuse and provoke. SacSix does it with wheatpaste, a sharp eye, and a sense of humor.

Mural by Keith Haring (1958–1990). He blurred the line between graffiti and art.

GRAFFITI: VERY OLD AND KIND OF OLD

Graffiti (from the Italian word for "scratch") has been a form of rebellion since ancient times. Archaeologists have uncovered graffiti that is vulgar (like today!) or political (like today!). In ancient Pompeii, which was destroyed in 79 AD when Mount Vesuvius erupted, one bit of graffiti translates to "Marcus Cerrinius for magistrate. Some people love him, some are loved by him, I can't stand him." It's a natural human impulse to mark up public property with opinions.

Anonymous artist Banksy stenciled and spray painted this piece in Nicholas Everitt Park as part of his August 2021 "Spraycation" along the eastern coast of England.

In New York City in the 1980s, graffiti art was going strong. Artists like Jean-Michel Basquiat and Keith Haring got their start tagging subways and buildings, often with political or social messages.

Currently, a British artist with the street name Banksy stencils his rascally art onto walls and buildings all over the world. With humor and strange juxtapositions, he questions authority. His identity remains a secret, and finding his work is almost a sport.

WHEATPASTING DOWNTOWN NYC

In my New York City neighborhood, the East Village, any walk becomes a treasure hunt for street art. The lampposts and mailboxes and walls are tagged with spray paint, stencil art, stickers, and wheatpaste posts. Wheatpaste has been around since ancient times. It's been used for bookbinding and papier-mâché. Wheatpaste is basically a flour-and-water mixture that forms a clear glue. You paint it onto a wall with a brush and then you can post something made of paper, big or small.

SacSix is a paper-and-wheatpaste artist whose posts I've seen around and loved for years. His work is colorful and funny, showing public figures in totally unexpected ways. SacSix is his street art name. Most street art is technically illegal. You're not allowed to deface public property in NYC, so SacSix (like Banksy) stays anonymous. I don't know who SacSix really is, but he agreed to answer my questions online.

SACSIX: BEGINNINGS

SacSix is from Miami, but came to NYC, where he worked in advertising. He says he found inspiration outside the office. "Going on long walks to find street art was my favorite thing to do in the city. The streets were my MoMA [Museum of Modern Art], or my Whitney [Museum of American Art]."

He began photographing street art he liked, posting it on social media with shoutouts to the artists. SacSix explains, street art "made me feel good. It made me smile. I just wanted to do that for other people. So in December 2015, I put up my first wheatpaste. I've been addicted to street art ever since. Since then, I quit my job in advertising and am now a full-time artist."

SacSix's summer of 2020 PSA mashing up Dr. Fauci and Mr. Spock. Note the Pigeon of Truth.

SACSIX AND POLITICS

I started noticing leaders like Abraham Lincoln, Kamala Harris, and Barack Obama pictured in the SacSix paste-ups. I ask him about these pieces as art-activism. He says, "Believe it or not, I try to stay out of politics. However, it's been harder and harder to remain silent. I do typically have a point of view in my political art. But I never twist anyone's arm or tell them they 'have to do this.'"

In the summer of 2020, I spotted a giant SacSix mural that made me chuckle. SacSix explains, "Many of my mashups consist of taking two familiar things and blending them together, creating an entirely new conversation or meaning." This one is a mashup featuring Dr. Anthony Fauci, the director of the US National Institute of Allergy and Infectious Diseases. He played a key role in advising Americans about the COVID-19 virus during the pandemic. In SacSix's rendering, Fauci is dressed as Mr. Spock, a very no-nonsense science-loving character from the original *Star Trek* TV series. That's Spock's native Vulcan hand salute, which means "live long and prosper." SacSix says, "Dr. Fauci as Spock, telling people to prosper by washing their hands, is just a fun way to think about the coronavirus. A way that you haven't previously." During a pandemic, washing your hands means life and death, so it's also a serious public service announcement. The summer when SacSix made the piece, Dr. Fauci was an advisor to President Trump, trying to get Trump to enlist science and logic to fight the virus's spread. But instead Trump spread misinformation. In the mural, Dr. Fauci has the Pigeon of Truth on his shoulder.

SacSix gives us a modern-day Abraham Lincoln in Pharrell Williams–style clothes. What would Lincoln think if he were here today?

MEASURING SUCCESS

People reach out to SacSix on social media and tell him they like his work. SacSix says, they "tell me how my art inspires them on their walks, and how it adds color and positivity to the city. Those DMs [direct messages] are why I do street art." He's giving back the inspiration he got years ago when he was an ad man walking around the city.

Sometimes people like SacSix's posts so much, they take them home. "People have gone to great lengths to steal the work, including bringing power tools to a location. It doesn't really bother me. I can always put up more. In fact, it just reinforces that I'm doing something right."

GIVE IT A TRY

Wheatpaste is cheap and easy to make. It's a glue made from just flour and water. A good starter recipe is 1 cup white flour to 4 cups water, whisked in a saucepot over heat, below boiling temperature. (There are dozens of recipes online that add salt or sugar or other ingredients. Explore.) You can draw, Photoshop, collage, or photocopy anything you want onto paper. Print out multiples. Then, since I cannot advocate breaking the law, pick a spot that's legal—like the side of your garage. Spread wheatpaste on a wall. Place the art on the wet wheatpaste. And seal it by brushing on more wheatpaste. Says SacSix, "One advantage to wheatpasting is that you can spend three to four hours in the studio making a piece, but it can take very little time to paste up."

Spotted July of 2021, SacSix's Donald Trump Junior in what looks like Chinese Communist gear

Chapter Fourteen
Zines: Be Seen Project

(2020–present)

Zines are small-circulation, self-published DIY magazines. Activist Mindy Tsonas Choi edits a zine where BIPOC artists contribute and speak out in "a radical snail-mail love bomb, delivered directly to your hands."

The late Justice Ruth Bader Ginsberg on the cover of BSP (Be Seen Project) zine

ZINE BACKSTORY

Zines started in the 1930s and '40s as sci-fi "fanzines." People typed or mimeographed them (mimeographs were a way of making copies with a machine that pushed ink through a stencil). When photocopy machines and copy shops came on the scene in the 1970s and '80s, zines hit a new stride. Since their creators had no publisher or authority to answer to, zines were usually

The first issue of *Bust*, made on a copy machine and stapled together in 1993

Mindy Tsonas Choi, zine editor, collage maker, and self-proclaimed radical belonging activist

cheeky and rebellious. Zines were big in the punk music scene in London, LA, and NYC in the 1980s.

I bonded with Be Seen Project (BSP) founder and zine editor, Mindy Tsonas Choi, over our love for a feminist-powered zine from 1993. It was a copied-and-stapled, black-and-white zine called *Bust*. It spoke to our young souls. At the time, it was radical to find a publication—however lo-fi—that celebrated women as smart and beautiful and political all in one place. *Bust* grew into a magazine that's still published today by the same founders.

BE SEEN PROJECT MISSION

The Be Seen Project also has a rad political mission: help BIPOC (Black, Indigenous, and People of Color) artists who are using their art for social justice and cultural change. Help amplify marginalized voices. Mindy explains, "If someone cannot see you to begin with, they cannot meet your needs." So Mindy started the Be Seen Project.

ORIGIN TALE

I ask Mindy what sparked this project. She says, "It's a direct response to what happened this year. Me losing my full-time job. The world coming to lockdown. Us facing this huge racial justice moment. Also needing justice for Asian Americans. It was the eye of the storm." She's talking about the year 2020. Mindy's job disappeared because she'd been teaching at art retreats that were no longer happening because the country was on lockdown to fight COVID. Then–President Trump was using anti-China slurs. Mindy says, "He was calling out a narrative that was harmful and racist. And we saw a rise in anti-Asian violence." Mindy is Korean. And then the murder of unarmed Black man George Floyd by police officers fueled protests nationwide.

Mindy wanted to take action. "It was a project I was simmering on. A lot of my work is about how being seen is such an important part of creating identity. It was time to meet the moment."

WHY A ZINE?

With her graphic design background, artistic talents, and love for paper collage, it was natural to start a zine. The Be Seen Project initiative includes fundraising, social media, a podcast, and more. But, Mindy says, "I really wanted something to put in people's hands. It made sense to go back to the zine roots. I specifically wanted to go and make it on the copy machine."

Mindy also wanted to send her support of BIPOC artists through the mail because "the USPS is under attack." 2020 was also an election year. And because of the COVID quarantine, mail-in ballots were more important than ever. President Trump was undermining the US Postal Service in order to undermine the election results. (It didn't work.)

THE JOY OF ZINE-ING

Mindy's voice sparkles when she talks about making her zines. Mindy says she loves "the connections made reaching out to artists to be part of it. I love to meet new creatives. Their stories and the things they are working on in their lives."

Another source of joy: editorial freedom. Mindy doesn't have to worry about sales or advertisers. The content of her zine is just 100 percent the message and artists she wants to send out to the world. And when she picks artists and contributors, she doesn't have to worry about how many online followers they have. Her main question is "Do they have work that resonates?"

COMMUNITY BUILDING

Mindy explains that zines are a great tool for "connecting and grassroots building." A zine is like a homegrown local paper, but with the news you personally want to share. Mindy says a fun bonus is "being able to connect other people through zines. I've met librarians and curators. There's definitely a zine revival happening." Does Mindy have any theories about that? Is it like music lovers who go back to vinyl because there's something to touch? She says, "I think it's the sense of going back to analog. It's the DIY. It's super accessible—pushes back against the bright and shiny production we see all the time."

PROUD ZINE MAMA

I think the sparkle in Mindy's voice is pride. The best kind. Pride from "really creating a space where it isn't hierarchical" and creating a platform for "marginalized voices that have been oppressed by the dominant narrative. Storytellers missing from the craftivist movement and the feminist movement."

That's an important reminder. The world of craftivists and feminists can have a lot of white forty-plus women (like me). Sometimes we need to just step back and listen to everybody else.

INSIDE THE BSP ZINE

In the debut issue of the *Be Seen Project* zine, Vol 1 (zines tend to have a Vol 1, 2, 3, etc. numbering system instead of issues and dates like magazines), there's a half page illustration by artist Janine Kwoh—aka Kwohtations. Mindy discovered Janine's work through her super-fun yet wise Kwohtations sticker art. sticker art. Says Mindy, "Everything in the BSP zine is BIPOC-created and activism-focused, so it fit the bill."

Kwohtations' zine entry is full of advice on how to be an activist and an ally. I noticed that the people she draws are not necessarily men or women or any certain race or age, which makes the message feel applicable to all.

Mindy's *Be Seen Project* zine helps BIPOC artists spread ideas and inspiration.

INTERSECTIONALITY

"The Future is Intersectional," says the crystal ball in Kwohtations' illustration. Intersectionality is a major theme throughout the Be Seen Project posts and literature. I ask Mindy to help explain it. "We all hold different identities. We can belong to different examples of those groups at the same time. We can talk about disability, age, marital status, [being a] child bearer, Black, queer. Intersectionality is the process of having the authority to claim who we are, not being identified as any one of those labels. We have multiple identities and complexity."

BABY'S FIRST ZINE

I ask Mindy to suggest a good starter project for a zine newcomer. And she does not hesitate to answer, "Oh, the classic eight-page zine. You make it with an eight-by-eleven piece of paper, pen, and a pair of scissors. You cut down the middle and it folds a perfect way. It ends up being pocket-sized." This sounds like an ideal craftivism project: handmade, simple, and it can carry a message. "Once you have your pages, the sky is the limit. Use whatever tools you want to play with." Cut and paste from magazines, use rubber stamps, watercolors, stickers. As for your zine's message, Mindy notes that, "it can be specific, or can be more broad. Can be subject-based, can be anything. Which I love."

Once you make a few zines, you can distribute them by snail-mailing them to friends or politicians (keep that post office in business!). You can leave a pile to give away at your local coffee shop or thumbtack a few to a bulletin board at school or anywhere people still have bulletin boards. Mindy also suggests starting a zine club of your own, "Maybe enlisting the help of an awesome teacher or troop leader. Making zines together and hosting zine swaps with other friends could be lots of fun. Collecting zines is a way to connect and broaden your world view. Seek and build community with like-minded zinesters. Community really helps support activism and craftivism!"

Artist Janine Kwoh, who's also a letterpress printer, made an illustration featured in Vol. 1 of the *BSP* zine.

Mindy's worktable and tools, as she makes some 8-page zines

HOW TO MAKE YOUR OWN 8-PAGE ZINE

1. Fold 8" x 11" piece of paper in half, the long way.
2. Fold in half again, the short way.
3. Fold in half one more time, the short way.
4. Open up paper to see pages. At this stage, you can mark the front and back covers and page numbers in pencil and erase those marks later. That's optional.
5. Fold paper in half, as shown. Cut from the folded edge, halfway across.
6. Open to show slit in the middle.
7. Fold again, the long way.
8. Push the two ends toward each other, to make the middle pop out.
9. Keep pushing further until it folds into a book. (Pro tip: If you mark your covers and pages at step 4, it's easier to see where everything lands for step 9. If you prefer to see hands doing this, there are many how-to videos online.)

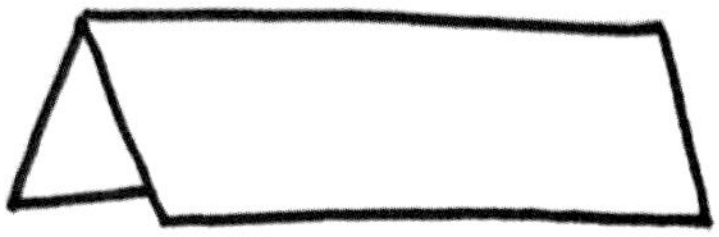

1 fold

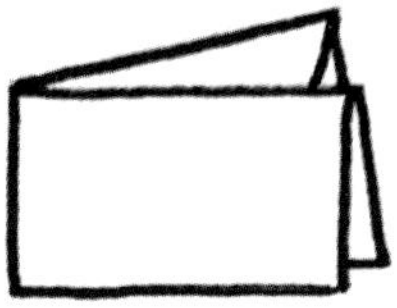

2 fold

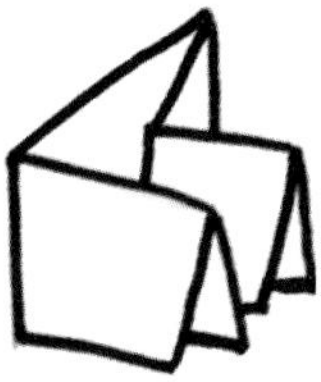

3 fold

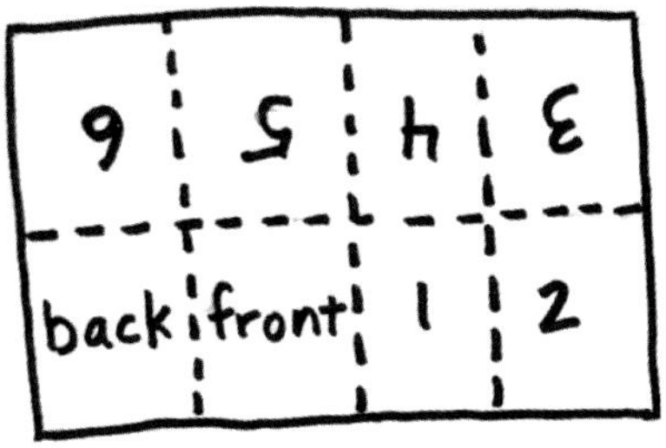

4 open up

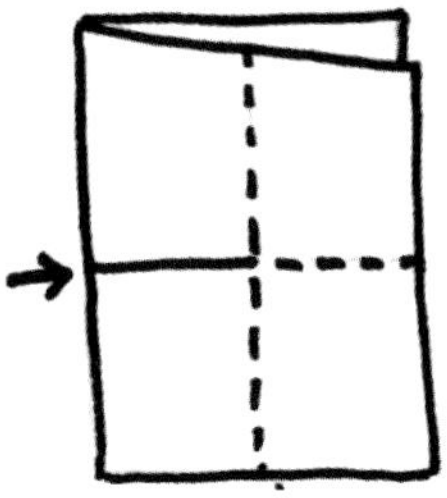

5 cut line

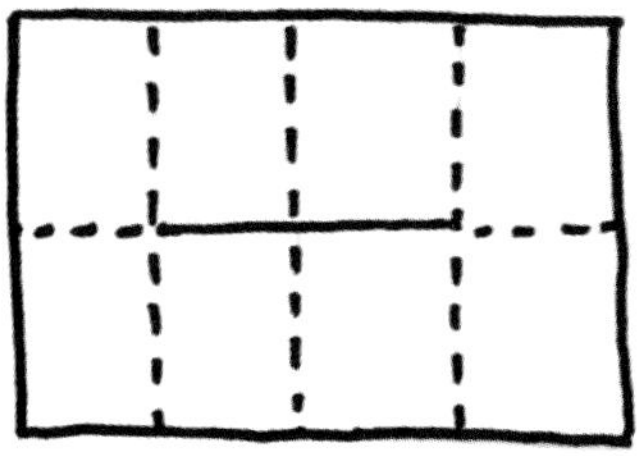

6 to create slit in the center

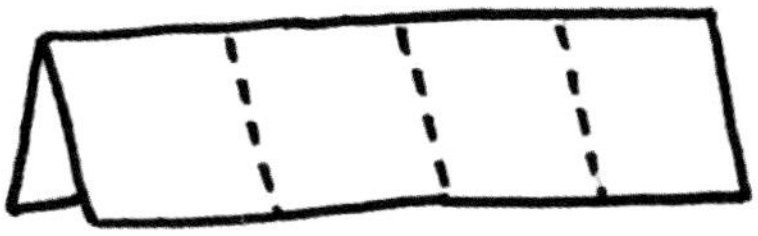

7 fold

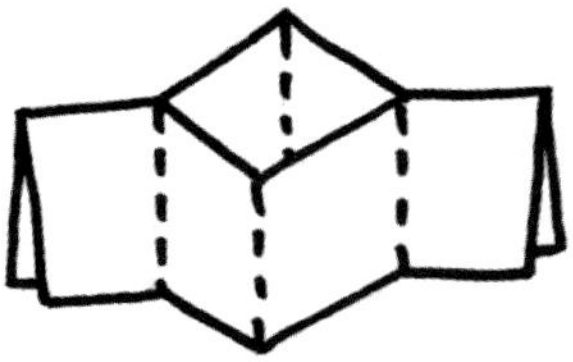

8 pop out middle

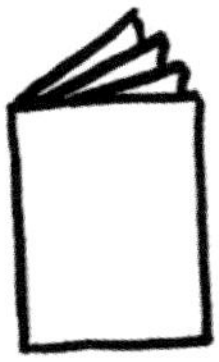

9 fold

Chapter Fifteen

Craftivist You: The Constitution of Crafts

Craftivism is art made by the people for the people—like a healthy democracy. Here are ten reasons to start your craft army of one.

WORDS INTO ACTION

After meeting these art-activists and seeing the gorgeous, inspiring things they've created for a cause, are you ready to tread down their paths? Or make new paths? Are you the type who'd rather fill a tire with sand to turn garbage into a house or sit quietly by the window with needle and thread to stitch your statement?

There are so many reasons to craft for a cause. In the spirit of patriotism, I mapped out ten of them. It's my Constitution of Crafts. (Note: Not legally binding.)

The Constitution of Crafts

Article 1.
Political crafting feels good, lifts the spirit.

Consider it anger management. When you're angry or frustrated, you feel it in your soul and also in your body. So to physically touch materials and transform them by hammering, knotting, poking with a needle—it just feels good. If you're a naturally restless person (like I am) you may find that the quiet repetition of knitting or embroidering calms and relaxes you. Making a giant stencil-and-spray-paint mess in your backyard can feel liberating. When you craft with a purpose like, "I'm sending this to my senator" or "There's someone who's cold and needs this hat," that purpose lifts your spirits and carries you along to the finish line. When you *do* finish, you feel proud. The power to create is power, indeed.

Article 2.
Political crafting can
be solitary.

Maybe you've never been an activist because you're not a joiner. Perhaps the idea of marching or protesting or being on a committee sounds annoying. Or too confrontational. That's fine. But then, how about sewing a protest quilt on a winter night while listening to podcasts or music? And then you auction off your quilt online and send the profits to your favorite cause. That's craftivism. And you never have to leave your house or shout rhyming slogans.

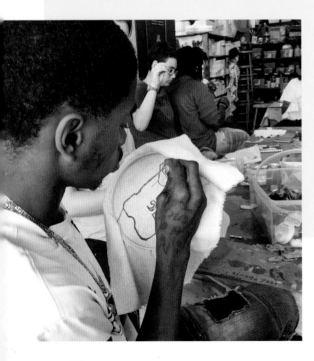

Article 3.
Political crafting can
be communal.

Though you are just one person, maybe you are naturally social and *want* to practice your activism with other humans. Maybe your current friends are getting on your nerves and you are ready to meet some new people. There's a long tradition of strangers and friends coming together to craft. From quilting bees to stitch-and-bitch knitting circles to barn raisings. Creating with fellow makers—online or in person—is an easy way to have a conversation, maybe even a new, refreshing conversation. Craft with a group, and that group can become a support system. All while they help get your knots unknotted or advise you on color choice. Plus, nothing bonds people together faster than a common enemy. So if you are embroidering a #NoFrackingWay quilt square in a stitch-along or painting a mural with a group, you'll probably make a friend.

Article 4.
Political crafting is not always sweet.

Handicrafts are traditionally cozy and soothing. Think of hand-made things you might see at a baby shower, like a bib with embroi-dered duckies carrying umbrellas. Cozy and soothing, yes? Sending a harsh message through (literally) soft materials makes people uncomfortable. They don't expect it. It's provocative. Isn't that the point of activism—to provoke in order to bring about change?

Article 5.
Political crafting is a chance to interrupt.

Craftivism—and maybe all activism—is a way to interrupt the norm. Just like a protest march interrupts the daily schedule of work and traffic to make a point. It interrupts the news cycle. On a smaller scale, art-activism can get you and those around you to break from habitual thinking. Art-activism interrupts the autopilot we all use to get through the day. It raises questions like "Hmm . . . Why do men speak up more than women in PTA meetings?" . . . "Why am I not afraid of police officers, while other people stress out around cops?" . . . "How much money does the person making me this hamburger get paid, and how can they live on that?" . . . "What's the harm in wasting water?" . . . "Who is Ahmaud Arbery?" If our embroidered postcards and quilts, and clay sculptures can interrupt the normal, then we can sit with the discomfort, and start to build a better normal.

Article 6.
Political crafting can raise money for a cause.

This is just practical. Fundraisers don't have to involve rich old white people wearing pearls. You don't need to throw a gala to get some green. You can run a table at a craft market. You can take custom orders from friends and family. You can sell your beautiful creations online (see Article 2) and donate the profits. I read about a bake sale for Planned Parenthood where all the cookies were shaped like vaginas. Craftivist bakers! Messages are great, but money is mighty.

Article 7.
Political crafting can broaden your skill set.

If you've vaguely thought about trying calligraphy or knitting or screen printing, then study up and dig in. Let a cause bigger than you be motivation. Find a class or a friend to teach you this new craft. Watch how-to videos. Set a clear goal, like making message cupcakes for a bake sale or stenciling a batch of political T-shirts for your friends to all wear together one day. Craftivism takes a hobby to a bigger, better place. No one skis to help the world. (Do they?)

Article 8.
Political crafting allows you to repurpose with purpose.

Even just turning some junk into art is a tiny way to change the world for the better. Whenever possible, I try to craft with found or used materials. There are so many things we use just once, and that's wasteful and harmful to the environment. So make a stencil out of your mom's used file folders and spray paint onto jeans from the thrift store. Steal your brother's old book bag and embroider slogans on it. Craftivism is an attempt to do good, so try not to add waste in the process.

Article 9.
Political crafting offers an opportunity to consider other POVs.

If you are putting a message out there, you will get feedback. If you stitch "My body is a temple, now keep your state out of my church!" onto a denim shirt, your hands will be tired because that slogan is long. But if you wear that shirt, you invite conversation—some supportive and maybe some hostile. But (within reason) that conversation could be interesting. Try to listen as much as you talk, hear another person's point of view, and don't expect to make a convert. Start a discussion, not a fight. Use good judgment. Craftivism can provide a way to come out of your political shell. And isn't that better than just reading tweets from like-minded friends?

Article 10.
Political crafting works well with humor.

Yes, you are angry and fired up, but if you can make people laugh, then you're getting into their heads. That's step one in opening a dialogue. So many good jokes come from voicing a difficult truth, from treading in taboo territory. You can break the ice and be brutally candid all at the same time. Why do you think so many Women's March signs are funny? Why do you think dictators hate satire? Humor also takes us back to Article 1 (Political crafting feels good). It feels great to laugh and get your anger out in the form of a joke that's funny because it's true.

Now go get your hands dirty! Make a statement, make a difference.

Project How-Tos

Project One
Human Billboard
Embroidery

THE EASIEST WAY TO PROTEST

Humans make great billboards. They walk around and do stuff, bringing their messages to school, work, band rehearsal, and grocery stores. Politicians and giant corporations use spokespeople to sell their messages all the time, so why can't you be one? Here's a way to embroider a message onto your back—or your friend's back—and show it around town.

Humans make great billboards.

SEWING PEP TALK

If lacing your sneakers is the closest you've ever come to sewing, that's okay. You can still embroider. If you can learn one stitch, then it's like having one pen to write. It's all you need. A secret advantage of embroidery is that you can easily pull out stitches and redo your work if you need to—unlike painting or ice sculpting. No one will ever know. They just see the finished product.

MATERIALS & TOOLS

- **DENIM JACKET**
  Or jeans vest, army jacket, heavy work shirt—something made of thick woven fabric. Not stretchy, not thin.

- **DISAPPEARING FABRIC PEN (for light-colored fabric)** or **CHALK PENCIL (for dark-colored fabric)**

- **EMBROIDERY FLOSS**

- **EMBROIDERY NEEDLE**

- **SCISSORS**

- **SHEER PAPER and PENCIL (optional)**
  For tracing images or words off the computer screen. Cheap printer paper works nicely in a pinch.

- **EMBROIDERY HOOP (optional)**
  When I embroider on thick fabric like denim, I don't use a hoop. But if you want a little more stability or just that Jane Austen-y feel of an embroidery hoop in your lap, holding the fabric taut, try one.

A template traced from a laptop image helped to draw a glacier. Icy embroidery floss colors are ready for stitching along the chalk pencil lines.

DIRECTIONS

1. Pick your message and image

I chose to embroider a glacier because I've never seen one. When Glacier National Park was established in 1910, there were around eighty glaciers. Now there are only twenty-five. Clear proof that climate change is real. I also think glaciers are beautiful.

2. Transfer image and words onto fabric

I often draw freehand with a disappearing fabric pen or a chalk pencil. I'm not an amazing artist, and you don't need to be, either.

In this case, I "cheated" and traced an image off my computer screen. I cut out the glacier shape and used it as a template to trace. I drew in the details and contours freehand, erasing often.

Chain stitch is great for lettering. It makes fat lines.

3. Embroider image

To prepare to stitch, cut a piece of embroidery floss about the length of your arm—any longer and it will get tangled. Thread your needle and tie a knot by the bottom. Any knot will do, since it won't show.

For basic clear, crisp lines, I love the backstitch. A backstitched line can be smooth or a little jerky and jagged, which I prefer for a glacier.

4. Embroider words

I save the words for last because sometimes while I am stitching the picture, I think of something better to say. For text, I like using a chain stitch because it's easy, goes quickly, and makes fat letters that people can read from far away.

5. Finish up

When ending a thread, bring it through to the wrong side of the piece, run your needle under the nearest stitch, and tie a knot any way you can.

Maybe stitch tiny little Xs to be snowflakes. Embroidery is like drawing with thread. Play until the work feels finished.

6. Share your work with the internet (optional)

If you make something you're proud of, snap a photo and post on social media. It's another way to spread your message. And maybe you'll inspire others to try making an embroidered billboard, too.

7. Put your work on a human and send it out into the world

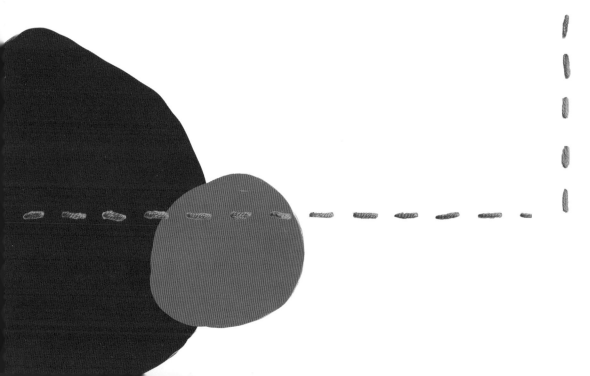

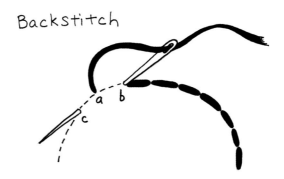

Backstitch

HOW TO BACKSTITCH

Bring your thread up through the fabric (a), then go back one stitch (b), then behind the fabric, you travel two stitch lengths forward to come up at (c). Enjoy the poetic beauty of one stitch back and then two stitches forward. Isn't life like that?

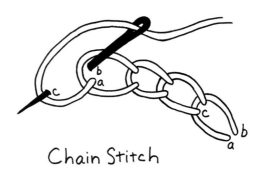

Chain Stitch

HOW TO CHAIN STITCH

Bring your thread up through the fabric (a), then go back down where you came up or very close to it (b). The thread will form a little loop. Then bring your needle up (c) to catch the loop. Pull the needle through and gently tighten the loop, but not too tight. Your new starting place for the next loop is (c). The loop-inside-loop pattern forms a chain.

Project Two

Spell-It-Out Bracelets

Beading

Beaded message bracelets are like bumper stickers for your wrist.

NOT FOR BABIES

A friend told me about these homemade bracelets that spell out big, powerful messages with tiny sweet letters you'd expect on a baby's ID bracelet or in a kindergarten art class. I tracked down the crafter, Cary L., and asked her to teach me how to make them. She said yes (obviously).

THE BACKSTORY OF THIS CRAFT FROM CARY L.

I have been doing crafts my whole life. My grandmother taught me to knit when I was six. I've knitted countless scarves, sewn many quilts, made bracelets and flowers from antique buttons, and decoupaged cigar boxes. I love creating something that didn't exist before, and bringing beauty into the world.

I have also devoted my life to social justice. My parents took me to demonstrations against the Vietnam War when I was a kid. They talked about fairness, the Civil Rights Movement, and the criminal justice system at the dinner table. After college, I worked for an organization founded by Ralph Nader [a longtime consumer advocate], and then I went to law school to become a public interest lawyer. I've been able to use my legal skills to protect people with HIV from discrimination in health insurance, get accessible trailers for people with disabilities in Louisiana and Mississippi after Hurricane Katrina, and get government agencies to send information in accessible formats to people who are visually impaired.

For a long time, crafts were a way to relax and take my mind off of work. The social justice issues I deal with at work can take years to fix. That can be frustrating. In contrast, most craft projects take much less time. I love the "the scarf is growing longer before my eyes" feeling that might take years for me to feel at work.

And then these two parts of my life came together. One day, I was very upset about things that were going on in the country, and I pulled out some alphabet beads and elastic thread and made a few bracelets expressing my outrage. I was already going to demonstrations and writing letters to politicians and giving money to organizations working on the issues. Now I had a new, fun way to express my views and share them with others. Soon, when I read the paper or watched the news, I was listening for phrases that I could use or modify for my bracelets. There are other benefits. They make great gifts, of course. Strangers notice the bracelets and ask me what they say—which can lead to interesting conversations, even new friendships. And small bracelets can be worn discreetly. Some people can't wear T-shirts with political messages to work or have a dress code at school, but they can wear a bracelet. Friends have excitedly told me about wearing their bracelets to work, hidden under the cuff of a sleeve. It's as if the bracelet reminds them of who they are and what they believe.

I hope you will try making bracelets and see if it gives you as much satisfaction as it gives me.

—Cary L.

Beading supplies can fit on a table. You can make bracelets while you watch TV.

MATERIALS & TOOLS

- **ALPHABET BEADS**
  6- or 7-millimeter round, flat, acrylic alphabet beads are the most common. Cube-shaped alphabet beads work, too.

- **OTHER BEADS**
  Beads to serve as spacers between words and to fill out the sides of the bracelet. Glass beads that are 3 or 4 millimeters in diameter are good, but really, any beads that can slide onto the elastic are worth trying.

- **ELASTIC THREAD**
  Thread that is .5 millimeters thick works best. This is thick enough to use without a needle, but thin enough to tie into a secure knot.

- **SCISSORS**

- **RULER or MEASURING TAPE**

- **HOUSEHOLD GLUE**

- **STORAGE BOXES WITH COMPARTMENTS (optional)**
  If you plan on making more than a few bracelets and you have a lot of alphabet beads, you may want some plastic boxes with compartments, so you can sort the alphabet beads by letter.

DIRECTIONS

1. Sort alphabet beads

Sorting beads is like prepping food for cooking. It may not be the most fun part and it takes a while, but doing it makes cooking go much faster. Separate the beads by letter. You can sort them into baggies or egg cartons or plastic containers with compartments.

2. Prepare elastic thread

Cut a piece of elastic thread to about fifteen inches. The bracelet will be shorter, but you need a few inches on each side to tie it together. Tie a double or triple knot a couple of inches from one end.

Plan out the whole bracelet
before you string a single bead.

3. Decide how big to make bracelet

If you are making the bracelet for a particular person, you can measure their wrist. Otherwise, since it's elastic you can guesstimate size. A good general guideline is:

- Small kid = 6 inches

- Big kid = 6.5–7 inches

- Adult woman = 7 inches

- Adult man = 8 inches

4. Decide what bracelet should say

This can be tricky, because many important, clever, or funny things are just too long to fit on a bracelet. You may need to find a shorter way to convey your message. "I am not your handmaid" can be "Not your handmaid." Punctuation beads do not exist! You just have letters and spaces to make your point.

On a bracelet for an adult woman, limit your message to twenty-three letters. Any more and the message will be unreadable or the bracelet will be too big.

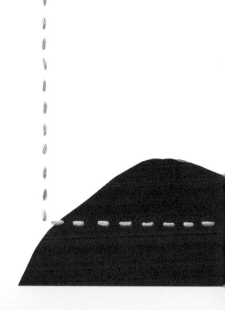

PRO TIP FROM CARY L.

Once you start beading messages, you'll quickly see that you need some letters more than others. Obviously you need a lot of Es, but you may be surprised how very, very much you need them. Fun fact: The letter E is used fifty-six times as often as the letter Q. But a bag of mixed alphabet beads often has as many Qs as Es— if not more. This means you have to buy more bags of beads to get those precious Es and other frequently used letters. Sometimes you can find bags of a single letter of the alphabet.

5. Pre-assemble bracelet

Lay out the words of your message. Then choose the spacer beads to go in between the words. Keeping the spacer beads smaller than the alphabet beads helps the message stand out. Play around with words and phrases. Larger beads on either side of the whole phrase can add emphasis like pretty brackets. Try to keep the message in the center of the bracelet with an equal amount of filler beads on either side. This will help keep the knot hidden in back. Use the ruler to check the length before you start stringing onto the elastic.

6. String bracelet

String the beads onto the elastic in the order you laid out. Measure the bracelet again. Add or subtract beads as needed. One bigger bead at the end will help hide the knot. Check to make sure that the alphabet beads are all right-side up, there are spacer beads between each word, and everything is spelled correctly. (Cary L. says, "I have made my share of bracelets that have upside-down alphabet beads and what I call 'beados'—beading typos.")

Work in progress. There's still time to turn around upside-down letters, add extra beads for length, switch colors.

To finish the bracelet, bring the two ends together and make a fresh new knot by tying the ends together three to five times. (You can ignore the knot you made earlier.) Put a tiny dot of glue on the knot and let it dry. Later, add one more dot of glue on the knot and snip off the ends of the elastic thread. Wear one or several bracelets out into the world, and let the conversations begin.

PRO TIP

Apply the dot of glue with a toothpick or something skinny so you don't get glue all over the other beads.

Project Three
Say It and Spray It

Stenciling

Stencils are great for making multiples.

THE JOY OF STENCILING

If craftivism is about getting a message out, then why not make multiples? Stenciling is a classic way to say something over and over and over. You can stencil on shirts, posters, art canvas, or even the basement door (with permission). How about a pile of T-shirts and totes for a flea market or yard sale? Stencil onto things you already have—like a raincoat, wooden crate, or throw pillow—and they feel new again.

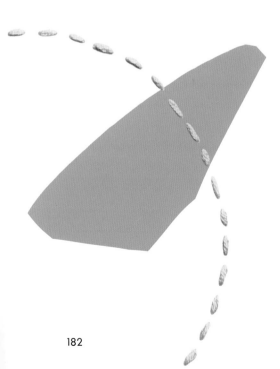

MATERIALS & TOOLS

- **CARDSTOCK**
  Manila folders work great.

- **PENCIL or BALLPOINT PEN**

- **NOTEBOOK PAPER or PRINTER PAPER**
  For stencil design

- **X-ACTO KNIFE or MEDICAL SCALPEL**

- **SELF-HEALING MAT or SHEET OF THICK CARDBOARD**
  A self-healing mat is a plastic work surface designed for safe cutting. Thick cardboard can work.

- **SPRAY PAINT**
  The kind that paints on wood and metal

- **NEWSPAPER or SCRAP PAPER**
  To block out spray paint spillover

- **FACE MASK and RUBBER GLOVES**
  Spray paint is toxic to your lungs and skin, so you need to work outdoors with mask and gloves.

- **MASKING TAPE**

- **WEIGHTS**
  Something that can get dirty, like soup cans or rocks

- **CLEAR TAPE (optional)**

- **LAPTOP (optional)**

- **COMPUTER PRINTER (optional)**

- **THINGS TO STENCIL ONTO**
  Cardboard, canvas, wood, or fabric that's not too thin. Basically anything that will receive paint.

Stenciling is messy but fun. You probably have a lot of the supplies already.

DIRECTIONS

1. Choose design and message

You can draw your design freehand or you can design it on your computer and make a printout. I like to use my laptop computer as a cheater's light box and trace onto paper.

IMPORTANT NOTE

Watch out for "floating" parts of your design. For example, the letter O as printed here has a floating middle. If you cut this O out with a blade, the oval in the middle will not stay. You'll just have a big empty oval, not a doughnut shape. Os, As, Ps, and other letters need to be broken into parts so nothing "floats" away. All designs and letters must connect to the main stencil sheet. If you are new to stenciling, keep it simple.

When I tried this project, I combined designs that I traced off my laptop. Then I printed out the text from my computer.

I wanted to do a take on the classic Jolly Roger skull and crossbones, with a cute baby chick, to remind people that when we eat animals, we are . . . eating animals.

A laptop computer can also be a light box for tracing.

I taped the printed text below my traced drawing.

2. Transfer design to cardstock

Lay your paper design over the card-stock and tape it in place. Working on a hard desk or table, trace the edges of your design with a pencil or ballpoint pen. Press hard! The design will etch into the cardstock. Repeat if necessary.

Press hard to etch design into cardstock underneath.

3. Cut out design with blade to form stencil

Please do this step slowly. Use the X-Acto blade or scalpel to cut out shapes and words etched into the cardstock. Keep extra fingers away from the blade. The negative cutout space will make the design.

Note how the letter *A* stays connected to the main stencil.

Spray paint with short, wispy strokes.

4. Prepare work area

Set up your workspace outside so you have good ventilation. Make sure your work surface is very flat. A bumpy surface means paint might sneak in where you don't want it to go. If you are planning to stencil a T-shirt or canvas or anything of value, try a practice stencil on paper or cardboard first. Get the feel of it.

5. Place stencil

Lay stencil design flat, and put weights (soup cans, rocks) on the corners to keep it still. Use newspaper or scrap paper to block the surrounding area from spray paint spillover (see photo). If you are stenciling onto fabric, put cardboard underneath the fabric so spray paint does not soak through.

6. Spray paint over stencil—very carefully!

Put on a mask to cover your nose and mouth. Put on thin latex rubber gloves to keep paint off your skin.

Shake paint can before you start. Make sure the spray nozzle is pointed away from you. Paint in short quick strokes, going across the stencil. Always keep the can moving as you spray. Spray thin wisps, not thick, goopy, drippy stripes. A pencil or chopstick can help hold the stencil down while you spray. Stop and shake the can often between spray strokes.

7. Let paint dry and remove stencil

Let the paint dry for at least three minutes. Remove weights and gently peel off stencil.

8. Repeat!

Try different surfaces. Try placing your stencil off-center or diagonally on a shirt or poster. If your stencil gets soggy or beat up, just make a fresh stencil by repeating steps two and three. Or try a brand-new design.

It's very satisfying to lift off the stencil and see the design.

Now What?

Crafting Change from Here On: Now What?

WHAT CAUSES DO YOU WANT TO SUPPORT?

Where do you get your information about the world? From newspapers . . . teachers . . . documentaries . . . comedians . . . social media . . . TV news . . . your parents . . . other people's parents? Use your best critical thinking. Consider the source. Passion is great, but be aware of the difference between facts and feelings. Is the news story stoking fear? Double-check data points. Are there even any checkable facts? They say it's good to get a second opinion from another doctor when you are sick, so too with the news.

Most of the craftivists in this book have an online presence and post projects that you can try. If their work does not speak to you, then find an organization or cause that you believe in. Ask like-minded friends or relatives if there are any charities or political groups they support. If you see a political T-shirt or pin or bumper sticker that intrigues you, ask about it. That's why they exist. (I just saw a bumper sticker that said "TALK BERNIE TO ME," meaning US senator Bernie Sanders.) Feel free to ask hard questions (like: "How can we reduce the need for gas and oil if everyone has a car?"). Welcome debate into your life.

MAKE STUFF TO HELP

I think crafting can help in at least four ways. (Also, I like lists.) You can 1) make crafts with a message for the public to see, 2) make crafts to send and show to people in power, 3) make crafts that directly help people in need—like knitting hats for soldiers or blankets for immigrants, and 4) make crafts to sell, and raise money for a cause.

If you are the social type, maybe host a crafting circle at your house with friends and delicious snacks. If you are part of an organization—a church, a temple, a mosque, a marching band, student government, book club, etc.—you might want to look into starting a craftivism group. Make it clear that all skill levels are welcome and prepare to teach the newbies.

LISTEN WITH AN OPEN MIND

I know that when I was a teenager, I had very strong feelings about right and wrong. I was sure I was on the side of Right and Justice. But now I see the gray area. When someone has an opposing view, ask yourself: What are they protecting? How will their life change if this law/issue/problem changes? Are they a monster? Probably not. It's unkind and unfair to write people off as idiots because they don't agree with you. You will not change minds unless you open your own mind. The golden rule is pretty good: Treat others as you would like to be treated.

Also remember: It's okay to feel opposing feelings at the same time, like . . . (positive) I love and believe in the US Constitution and (negative) I am mad at the Constitution for not protecting women more. (How is it possible that we have not passed an Equal Rights for Women Amendment? HOW?!?!?)

DON'T STOP BEING AN ACTIVIST

The work of activism is ongoing. It's like weeding a garden: You can't just sit back and say you're done. Take a break and rest if you need to. Support others who are helping. But be ready to get in there again. Your country needs you.

ACKNOWLEDGMENTS

Thank you, Joy Peskin, my wise and patient editor. The book we dreamed up at the 2017 Women's March came true! Your guidance was key to the shape, contents, and scope of our book-baby! To designer Trisha Previte for making this come alive with color and energy. To Mallory Grigg for getting the art and design over the finish line. Production editor Ilana Worrell for keeping it all together and moving! To Asia Harden and Jamie Chen for following up on a million details, like human safety nets. To my literary agent, Sarah Lazin, for decades of support, and for declaring this book "hopeful." Thank you, Cara Levine. You were the first artist I interviewed, and our discussion influenced the rest of the book. To Shannon Downey, for helping me to see embroidery as powerful, also for your time and generous intros to other craftivists. Thanks to all the other artists who opened up about their work: Melissa Blount, Jayna Zweiman, Mike Reynolds, Guillermo Galindo, Sara Trail, Becca Rea-Holloway, Mindy Tsonas Choi, Alyssa Garcia, SacSix, Janine Kwoh, and Ekaette Ekong. Thanks to the scholars and experts who helped me understand the past: Susan Strawn, Mariah Gruner, and Julie Rhoad. Thanks to photographers Richard Misrach, Gloria Araya, Susan Donaldson, Shaun Coomer. People who helped me get materials and permissions: Lauren Anderson, Roddy Williams, Marvin Taylor, Stephanie Valencia, Lauren Black, Marcelle Karp. To Cary L. for sharing her crafting. Hanna Shykind for modeling. Illustrator Kate Burrascano for her beautiful work. To my cheerleaders: Kathy Ebel, Robin Sayers, Nancy Berkowitz Kaplan, Deirdre Cossman, Charlie Schroder, Faith Salie, Deanna Storey, Trish Goodwin, Jo Honig, Dan Price, Lyuba Konopasek. And thanks to my encouraging parents: Paula Davidsen, Richard Vitkus, and Ann Allison. To my sweet and talented boyfriend, Stephen Murello, who watched our kids while I worked and took beautiful photos for the book. And to my daughters, Matilda and Sadie—keep making things!

IMAGE CREDITS

Embroidery elements throughout (pincushion, stitching): Ashley Wong; viii: Stephen Murello; x: Jessica Vitkus; xi: Susan Donaldson; xiv: Colorful yarns for embroidery © Barbara Neveu/Shutterstock; 2: Sean Su (Instagram @SeanSuPhoto); 3: Bill Burlingham; 7: Kate Burrascano; 8: Ben Blount; 9, 10: Jessica Vitkus; 12, 13: Shannon Downey aka Badass Cross Stitch; 15: Gloria Araya (Instagram @GloriaArayaPhotography); 16 (left): Eva Griffin-Stolbach; 16 (right), 17: Shannon Downey aka Badass Cross Stitch; 18: Mark Germain; 22: Wool yarn on shelves © Simon Russell/Getty Images; 25: Library of Congress, Prints & Photographs Division, LC-USZC4-9863; 26: Courtesy of Susan Strawn; 28: Library of Congress, Prints & Photographs Division, LC-DIG-ggbain-24312; 29: Kate Burrascano; 31: G.E. Mathios, Waterbury, Conn.; 33: Work Projects Administration for the City of New York. War Services; 38–39: Brian M.K. Allen; 41: Kat Coyle; 43: Abira Ali; 47 (both): Jessica Vitkus; 49: *The Gates*, by Christo and Jeanne-Claude, Central Park 2005; 50: C.J. Lind; 52: Bottle wall © IRC/Shutterstock; 54, 56 (both), 57, 60: Earthship Biotecture; 64: Guillermo Galindo Angel Exterminador (Exterminating Angel) performance at Schrin Kunsthalle, Frankfurt, Germany, 2019; 66: Carol M. Highsmith Archive, Library of Congress, Prints & Photographs Division; 68: Richard Misrach; 70 (top): Guillermo Galindo; 70 (bottom): Richard Misrach; 74: Cara Levine; 76: Shay Myerson; 77, 78, 79, 82, 83, 84: Cara Levine; 86: Geometric quilt © oxygen/Getty Images; 89: Library of Congress, Prints & Photographs Division, LC-DIG-npcc-20403; 90, 91: Courtesy of Historic New England, gift of Mrs. Edward M. Harris, 1923.597; 94: Dr. Mariah Gruner; 98: The New York Public Library, UUID a2abf0a0-c6cd-012f-8277-58d385a7bc34; 100: Division of Cultural and Community Life, National Museum of American History, Smithsonian Institution; 101: Virginia Vivier; 103: Carol M. Highsmith Archive, Library of Congress, Prints & Photographs Division; 104: Robin Sayers; 105 (both): Jessica Vitkus; 106: Kate Burrascano; 108, 109, 110: National AIDS Memorial; 117: Social Justice Sewing Academy; 118: Jessica Vitkus; 119, 120, 123, 125: Social Justice Sewing Academy; 128: Street art graffiti © A_Lesik/Shutterstock; 130: Becca Rea-Holloway; 132: Rhys Tucker; 134, 137: Becca Rea-Holloway; 138: Las Fotos Project; 139: Dorothea Lange, Library of Congress Prints & Photographs Division; 140: Las Fotos Project; 141, 143, 144: Las Fotos Project; 146: Camilo J. Vergara; 147: Shaun Coomer (Instagram @shauncoomer_); 148, 150, 151: Jessica Vitkus; 152: Mindy Tsonas Choi; 153 (left): Marcelle Karp; 153 (right): Mindy Tsonas Choi; 156: Jessica Vitkus; 157: Janine Kwoh; 158: Mindy Tsonas Choi; 159: Jessica Vitkus; 160: Cara Levine; 162: Shannon Downey aka Badass Cross Stitch; 163: Carol M. Highsmith Archive, Library of Congress, Prints & Photographs Division; 164: Social Justice Sewing Academy; 165: Becca Rea-Holloway; 167: Shannon Downey aka Badass Cross Stitch; 169, 170: Jessica Vitkus; 171: Stephen Murello; 173 (both), 174, 177, 178, 180, 181, 182: Jessica Vitkus; 183: Stephen Murello; 184 (both): Jessica Vitkus; 185 (both), 186, 187: Stephen Murello; 194: Jessica Vitkus

ABOUT THE AUTHOR

Jessica Vitkus works in television, covering politics every day. She produced for *The Daily Show with Jon Stewart* and *The Late Show with Stephen Colbert*. Jessica is a lifelong, self-taught crafter. Her specialty is embroidery, but she's tried just about every handmaking medium from metalwork to mosaics to paper collage. Jessica wrote about design and crafts for Martha Stewart's *Living* magazine, then wrote her own project book, *AlternaCrafts*. She hopes the revolution will be handcrafted, and wishes that every single citizen handmade at least one thing a year. Jessica lives in NYC's East Village with her cinematographer boyfriend and twin daughters.